THE MOTHER KITCHEN

Timeless Recipes from Old Italy

RENÉE GALIOTO

EDITED BY CAROL WHITE

RENÉE GALIOTO PRODUCTIONS INC.

TORONTO 1980

*This cookbook
is dedicated to David Ernest Jones
whose support and faith in me
has made it all possible.*

The Mother Kitchen: Timeless Recipes from Old Italy.
Copyright © 1980 by Renée Galioto Productions Inc. All rights reserved.
Printed in Canada. No part of this book may be used or reproduced
in any manner whatsoever without written permission except in the case
of brief quotations embodied in critical articles and reviews.
For information write to: Renée Galioto Productions, Inc.,
P.O. Box 480, Richmond Hill, Ontario L4C 4Y8.

Printed at the University of Toronto Press
ISBN 0-919281-00-1

Canadian Cataloguing in Publication Data

Galioto, Renée.
  The mother kitchen

ISBN 0-919281-00-1

1. Cookery, Italian.   I. White, Carol.   II. Title.
TX723.G34   641.5945   C81-094043-4

CONTENTS

ACKNOWLEDGEMENTS

I wish to extend a sincere thanks to the people who made this book a reality: My dear husband, Vito, who assisted invaluably in research and translation; Monsignor Tomasso Papa of Alcamo, Sicily, who filled in many gaps in my research; my dear friend Rena Santacapita, whose help and enthusiasm have been a mainstay; Bob Stevenson and Mary Phillips, whose encouragement and assistance enabled me to put the project in motion; Krystyna Szpilewicz, for typing the manuscript; and Janet and Joyce Jones, for all their support.

Greatly appreciated for their generous supply of props for photography were: Unico Foods Limited, DeCecco di Fillippo, Gallo Olive Oil, Moulinex Canada Ltd., Silton Importing Ltd., Maestro Foods Ltd. and Carolina Cheese Ltd.

I would also acknowledge the extraordinary work of the staff of University of Toronto Press and those listed below, who made it possible to produce this book in record time.

EDITOR
Carol White

PRODUCTION COORDINATOR
Andrew P. Jones

FOOD PHOTOGRAPHY
Ken Bell

DESIGN
Peter Moulding

SPECIAL CONSULTANTS
Jim White, Food Editor, Toronto Star
David E. Jones, Business Administrator,
Hagerman, Jones & Company Limited

ILLUSTRATIONS

PREFACE

For most people, Italian cuisine conjures up images of fettuccine Alfredo, veal Marsala or Neapolitan pizza. Certainly each is undeniably Italian. But even more than the blend of its traditional ingredients, Italian cooking is the source of every cuisine in the Western world: The Mother Kitchen.

As far back as 1900 B.C., the Phoenicians had set sail to all parts of the Mediterranean from their Syrian homeland. They established trading posts and colonies wherever they could, and by 1000 B.C. had founded such cities as Nuero and Cagliari in Sardinia and Marsala and Palermo in northwestern Sicily. As they traveled, they shared their knowledge of cooking, aided by Babylonian weights and measures and the alphabet we use today.

By 800 B.C., the Phoenicians had founded the North African city of Carthage, soon to become the capital of a new empire. The Greeks, in the meantime, had extended their empire to southern and eastern Sicily, establishing colonies at Syracuse, Catania, Messina and Selenunti. The resulting interplay between the Phoenicians and the Greeks and their contact with other neighboring cultures accelerated the development of fine cooking as an art.

From this culinary mosaic, The Mother Kitchen evolved with Syracuse at her centre. By 500 B.C., Syracuse had become the gastronomical mecca of the ancient world. When the Romans captured it from the Carthaginians 300 years later, they quickly recognized the superiority of its cooks. Afterward, when the Romans proclaimed Sicily their first province, enslaved Sicilian and Sardinian cooks were hauled off to the kitchens of Roman nobility.

The first Romans were shepherds and their diet consisted largely of meat and milk. They became skillful cheesemakers (and still are) and proficient producers of salt. Before long, salt became the basis for international trade as well as an important ingredient in The Mother Kitchen. The Via Salaria, or Salt Road, was built especially for carrying salt to the far reaches of the growing empire, and in turn, for bringing to Rome every conceivable foodstuff of the day.

Now these skilled slaves were called on to cater the great Roman banquets, a task requiring great ingenuity. They drew from The Mother Kitchen to create these extravaganzas. The Roman Empire effectively carried these basic cooking skills to every outpost of the conquered nations and exposed The Mother Kitchen to the wealth of cooking traditions within its far-reaching borders.

But then the empire fell. In the fifth century A.D., Italy was overrun by barbaric hordes and the glory of Rome was no more. The vast knowledge of culinary art appeared headed for oblivion. Food became a hand-to-mouth affair, with little attention to culinary refinements.

All was not lost, though. Throughout the Dark Ages which followed, Catholic monasteries retained the culinary writings and even added scope with new methods of preserving food.

During the next six or seven centuries, Italy became a patchwork of city-states, with the populace clustered around the fortresses of feudal lords. With trade at a standstill and food supplies scarce, diets for rich and poor alike were kept simple and unimaginative.

Finally in the thirteenth century A.D., the light of the Renaissance shone and The Mother Kitchen began to flourish. Trade routes, opened by the Crusaders, carried spices, sugarcane and fruits from the East. The city-states, especially strategic seaports, became noted for particular foods, determined by what could be grown locally or gained through barter.

As foreign relations developed among the nations of Europe, The Mother Kitchen acquired added importance. International diplomacy became an extension of an embassy's social knowhow, and specifically its cuisine. The ambassador who could entertain most successfully had the greatest influence at court. Consequently, the Italian ambassadors, noted for their culinary prowess, made a lasting impression on the culture of the other European countries.

The city of Florence is particularly worthy of note. During the Middle Ages, Florence became an international textile and finance center. The city was ruled by the Medici family, noted throughout the continent for its wealth, political prestige and love of the arts.

In 1533, Catherine di Medici married into the royal family of France and brought with her a team of Florentine chefs. Her husband was duly crowned Henry II and The Mother Kitchen was firmly rooted from that day on. In fact, for the next 200 years, French aristocrats used only Italian chefs in their kitchens.

As the New World opened up, European emigrants carried The Mother Kitchen to the Americas. At the same time, native American foods such as tomatoes, yellow corn, artichokes and potatoes were carried back by the explorers and transformed Italian cuisine into what it is today.

On the following pages, I have attempted to provide from my research a representative collection of authentic Italian recipes that geographically span the entire country. The recipes are of sufficient variety that you may prepare snack or feast; simple luncheon or elegant banquet.

The dishes are arranged in the same order that they appear in a full-course Italian meal: antipasti, first course (soup, pasta, rice, polenta), second course (meat, fish, game, vegetables), third course (salad) and desserts. There are also sections on sauces and single-course dishes.

It is my deepest hope that these recipes will provide a practical means of getting the most from your daily bread; and at the same time, foster a deeper understanding and appreciation for the heritage of Italian cooking: The Mother Kitchen.

Renée Galioto
November 1980

HOW I COOK

All cooks have their own way of doing things. Here are some of my tried and tested techniques that will work for you too.

Butter

I prefer to cook with clarified butter, which I store at room temperature in a covered container next to my stove.

To clarify butter, place a 500-g (1-pound) block of salted or unsalted butter in a saucepan over low heat until melted. Remove from heat and allow to sit a few minutes, until you can skim the fat off the top. Pour the clear liquid into a container, discarding the solids that have settled to the bottom. Clarified butter kept liquid (room temperature) is much easier to measure and combines well with other ingredients.

Many of my recipes call for sweet or unsalted butter. Sweet butter has a more delicate flavor and does not alter the texture of meats when sautéeing. Salt, on the other hand, tends to toughen meats and alters the taste.

Anchovies

Since salt is an integral part of fine cooking, the natural saltiness of the anchovy has made it a highly respected condiment. Although anchovies are not required in most of the dishes they appear in, their distinct flavor is a part of Italian cooking, and the true Italian taste is lost without them. You can reduce or increase the quantity of anchovies in a recipe according to taste.

Be sure not to substitute cocktail anchovy preparations for plain anchovy fillets, since they are highly seasoned and will distort the recipe.

Store anchovies in the oil they were packed in and don't keep for more than a week, since they become stale and unnaturally salty.

Vinegar

Red wine vinegar has a very distinct flavor, preferred to other vinegars, and is called for exclusively in these recipes. Italian cooking is based on the grape, and so wine is used frequently.

Do not substitute cider vinegar, since the fermentation of apple is quite different and the desired flavor will be lost. If you are using vinegar concentrate, simply water it down to its proper strength.

Do not use red wine vinegar in white sauces because it discolors them. Instead, use white wine vinegar, which you can make yourself by allowing leftover white wine to sit out, uncorked, at room temperature. The technique can also be used to make red wine vinegar simply by starting with red wine.

Pasta

Use only the best quality pasta you can find. Pasta should be made from hard-wheat flour, or it will be sticky and mushy. It should also be cooked properly. Always use plenty of water. My pasta pot is a five-litre (five-quart) cauldron that I fill two-thirds full with water. Bring to a rapid boil and throw in a handful of coarse pickling salt. When the water returns to a fast boil, drop in the pasta and stir immediately with a wooden spoon to keep it separated. Cook covered with the wooden spoon keeping the lid open just a crack and let boil as rapidly as possible without splashing all over your stove.

Stir frequently to prevent pasta from sticking to the bottom and to prevent the starch from settling on the pasta. When cooked to desired tenderness, add a cup of cold water to the pot, remove from heat and empty into a colander. Drain well, return pasta to pot and mix in a generous dab of butter. Allow to sit, covered, a few minutes on the cooling burner, and serve. This way pasta is flavored and the butter coating prevents it from sticking together.

Rice

Rice is perfectly cooked when it is *resotto all'onda*, or "like a wave." In other words, the surface ripples indicate the grains of rice are not sticking together, but are moist and succulent.

The round-grain rice grown in the Po Valley of Lombardy is the best for authentic Italian cooking and can be purchased at most specialty stores. Untreated long-grain rice is the next choice and gives a better flavor and texture than instant rice.

Polenta

Italian polenta is a finer grained cornmeal than the North American variety and I prefer it. If you use domestic cornmeal, sift it first.

To cook polenta, heat required amount of water and salt and bring to a boil. Mix polenta first with enough cold water to make it runny and then pour into boiling water in a thin steady stream, stirring constantly. Stir until mixture is smooth, reduce heat to a low boil and cover. Stir intermittently for 20 minutes, or until polenta no longer tastes doughy.

When I need to make a batch ahead of time, I pour the cooked polenta into a greased loaf pan and let cool into a solid loaf. I then refrigerate and reheat in the oven before removing from pan. Use fine string, a cheese slicer or knife to cut into individual portions.

My family enjoys polenta with chicken livers or *sugo* (any gravy or sauce). If kept for several days, fry polenta in slices using garlic-seasoned olive oil and serve in place of potatoes or pasta. Polenta makes a wonderful luncheon dish with leftover gravy from a roast.

Cheese

Try to use the required cheese for recipes. Most Italian cheeses are readily available in North America. It is important to buy cheeses that are fresh and grate them yourself whenever possible.

Imported Parmesan is definitely superior to North American brands because of its special curing. Domestic brands of ricotta, made from the milk of goats (the best) or cows, are quite good and appear in most supermarkets. If not available, use a moist cottage cheese, or for desserts, use cream cheese.

Romano or pecorino cheese can be substituted for Parmesan in a pinch, but use less because they are sharper in flavor. There's really no substitute for mozzarella, which you shouldn't have trouble finding. A satisfactory substitute for cacciocavallo is old cheddar.

Prepared meats

Northern Italy is noted for its mild, sweet sausage while the southern Italian sausage is hot and spicy. Use either, according to your taste, but both are different than domestic sausage in texture as well as seasoning. If you need a substitute, use fresh farmer's sausage with extra salt and pepper.

Pancetta is a salt-cured pork similar to back bacon, a reasonable substitute. Don't substitute side bacon, however, which is smoke-cured and quite different.

Prosciutto is a piquant, spiced meat that has no available meat substitute. Although it's expensive and available only at specialty shops, it's worth buying. Prosciutto imported from Italy is definitely the best, but domestic brands are also good. Prosciutto should not be too fatty and should be cut in paper-thin slices.

Fish

Fish is easily overcooked because the texture is very fine. The Canadian fisheries department has a good rule of thumb: Lay the fish on a flat surface and measure at its thickest point. Then allow 10 minutes of cooking time for every 2 cm (just under 1 inch) of thickness, regardless of method or whether the fish is in fillets, steaks or left whole.

Tomatoes

Sun-ripened tomatoes are available for only part of the year, but hot-house varieties are poor substitutes. Use canned plum tomatoes (drained) instead. These have fewer seeds than domestic types and are lightly seasoned with basil to give a full-bodied flavor.

Wines

Dry vermouth, white and red Marsala, dry white wine and red wine vinegar comprise my kitchen "first-aid kit." If used skillfully, they can turn the mundane into something special and hide a throng of errors.

Marsala is a blend of dry white wine, distilled wine (brandy) and wine concentrates, all from the Trapine and Marsala regions of Sicily. Including the extended periods of rest between stages, Marsala wine takes four years to mature. Consequently, there are no real substitutes. But in a pinch, a good dry sherry or vermouth can have a satisfactory result. There are suitable domestic varieties of vermouth, white wine and red table wines. Just remember that if a wine is not good enough to drink, it is not good enough to cook with.

Measurements

Because Italian cooking is an art, not a science, it is very difficult to give precise measurements. Individual tastes differ enormously. I would far rather express quantities as "use a few of this, a handful of that," and let the reader adapt accordingly. But of course, we want to accommodate the beginner as well as experienced cook and so, as frequently as possible, I have provided definite quantities.

Since Canada is now on the metric system, I have given the first measurement in metric terms, rounded to the nearest unit of 25 in most cases. Imperial equivalents (which are not direct conversions, but adaptations) are given in the right-hand column.

For those of you who haven't used metric measurements before, I want to stress that although they may look more complicated, they are far easier to use, once you start working with them. All you need to buy is a new set of measuring cups and spoons.

ANTIPASTI

The antipasti (plural of antipasto) are appetizers or hors d'oeuvres that are served before the meal. Originally this precourse was served as a means of keeping the guests happy while the cook was busily putting the finishing touches on the meal. Antipasti can be simple, such as a platter of cold cuts, deviled eggs or fried cheese bits; or more elegant, such as wine-steeped cantaloupe or stuffed mushrooms. Glance through the following pages and make your own selection of mouth-watering anti-pasti.

Devilled Eggs
UOVA RIPIENE

6		hard-cooked eggs	
		Juice of 1 onion	
		Salt and freshly ground pepper	
30–60	mL	béchamel sauce OR mayonnaise	2–4 tablespoons
		Few drops of olive oil	
		Paprika OR parsley OR anchovies	
		OR capers (optional)	

1. Cut eggs in half lengthwise. Remove yolks.

2. Combine yolks, onion juice, salt and pepper to taste and just enough béchamel sauce to bind mixture together.

3. Add oil, drop by drop, mixing frequently until mixture is creamy.

4. Fill egg whites with the mixture. Decorate with paprika, parsley, anchovies or capers.

Makes 12 devilled eggs

Wine-steeped Cantaloupe
MELONE AL MARSALA

Cantaloupe originated in Cantalupo, near Rome.

3		**medium-sized cantaloupe**	
375	**mL**	**Marsala wine**	1½ cups

1. Leaving each melon whole, cut out enough from one end of each to scoop out the seeds. Save the pieces removed.

2. Fill each cavity with 125 mL (½ cup) of wine.

3. Put the tops back on and marinate for several hours or overnight. Trim a small piece off each bottom if necessary to enable melons to stand upright.

4. Serve melon in halves, wedges or balls with wine marinade poured on top.

Makes 4 to 6 servings

Stuffed Mushrooms
FUNGHI RIPIENI

These make a delightful antipasto or a tasty side dish with turkey or pheasant.

12		**large fresh mushrooms with caps at least 5–8 cm in diameter**	2–3 inches
125	**mL**	**melted sweet butter**	½ cup
		Salt and freshly ground pepper	
15	**mL**	**olive oil**	1 tablespoon
45	**mL**	**finely chopped onion**	3 tablespoons
45	**mL**	**finely chopped green onion**	3 tablespoons
50	**mL**	**dry Marsala wine**	¼ cup
45	**mL**	**unflavored white bread crumbs**	3 tablespoons
125	**mL**	**grated Swiss Emmenthal cheese**	½ cup
50	**mL**	**grated Parmesan cheese**	¼ cup
50	**mL**	**fresh chopped parsley**	¼ cup
30–45	**mL**	**heavy cream**	2–3 tablespoons

1. Preheat oven to 190°C (375°F).

2. Cut off mushroom stems and chop finely. Squeeze chopped stems tightly in a clean tea towel to remove excess moisture. Set aside for later use.

3. Brush top and bottom of mushroom caps with 45 mL (3 tablespoons) melted butter. Place hollow sides up in a lightly buttered, shallow baking pan. Season lightly with salt and pepper.

4. Heat 30 mL (2 tablespoons) of the melted butter with all the olive oil in a saucepan and sauté onions for 3 to 4 minutes without browning. Add green onions and chopped mushroom stems and sauté over moderately high heat for 6 to 8 minutes. Add Marsala wine and cook rapidly until liquid is almost evaporated.

5. In a medium-sized bowl mix together the bread crumbs, half the grated Emmenthal, all the grated Parmesan, parsley and salt and pepper to taste. Stir bread crumb mixture into onion-mushroom mixture.

6. Blend in heavy cream, 15 mL (1 tablespoon) at a time, until the stuffing mixture is moist, but stiff enough to hold its shape in a spoon. Correct seasoning if necessary.

7. Fill mushroon caps with the stuffing. Top each with a sprinkle of the remaining Emmenthal and a few drops of the remaining melted butter.

8. Bake the stuffed mushrooms in the top third of the oven until caps are tender and the stuffing is lightly browned on top (about 15 to 20 minutes).

Makes 12 large stuffed mushrooms

Ricotta Balls
POLPETTE DI RICOTTA

500	g	ricotta cheese	1 pound
45	mL	grated Parmesan cheese	3 tablespoons
45	mL	all-purpose flour	3 tablespoons
		Salt and freshly ground pepper	
15	mL	fresh chopped parsley	1 tablespoon
2		eggs, beaten	
		Oil and butter for frying	
250	mL	cold tomato sauce (see page 104)	1 cup

1. Press ricotta cheese through a sieve into a mixing bowl. Add Parmesan cheese, flour, salt and pepper to taste, parsley and eggs. Mix well. (Or use a blender or food processor and process until smooth and creamy.)

2. Place mixture on a floured surface and knead lightly until dough holds together and is no longer sticky (3 to 5 minutes). (If mixture isn't firm enough to handle, add a little more flour and knead well.)

3. Keeping surface well floured, shape dough into walnut-sized balls, about 16 in total.

4. Fill a frying pan ¾-cm (¼-inch) deep with mixture of half oil and half butter and over moderate heat fry cheese balls until golden on all sides. Drain on paper toweling.

5. Pile balls on a serving dish. Serve with tomato sauce as a dip.

Makes 16 walnut-sized balls

Eggplant Salad
CAPONATA

500	g	unpeeled eggplant, cubed	1 pound
		Oil for frying	
3		stalks celery, chopped	
1		onion, chopped	
450	g	tomatoes, peeled and chopped	1 pound
45	mL	wine vinegar	3 tablespoons
30	mL	sugar	2 tablespoons
		Salt	
15	mL	capers	1 tablespoon
125	mL	pickled green olives, drained and pitted	½ cup
		Chopped toasted almonds (optional)	

1. Fry eggplant in oil until golden brown. Drain and set aside.

2. In oil eggplant was fried in, sauté celery and onion for 5 minutes.

3. Add tomatoes, vinegar, sugar and salt to taste and let simmer uncovered until celery is tender (about 10 minutes).

4. Add eggplant, capers and olives. Stir to blend and simmer uncovered an additional 10 minutes. Serve hot, or chill and serve cold the next day. If served cold, chopped toasted almonds may be added.

Makes 4 to 6 servings

Fried Cheese Bits

FORMAGGIO FRITTI

This recipe can be made with any cheese that can be grated. Experiment with a few different varieties to see which you like best.

125	mL	all-purpose flour	½ cup
		Pinch of salt	
75	mL	grated cacciocavallo OR cheddar OR cheese of your choice	5 tablespoons
15	mL	butter	1 tablespoon
1		egg, beaten	
		Cold milk (optional)	
		Oil for deep frying	

1. Mix together flour, salt and grated cheese. Cut in butter.

2. Add the egg and form a dough, working with a fork or your hands until dough is thoroughly mixed and pliable. Add a little cold milk if too dry. (Dough should be moist enough to adhere to itself if made into rolls.)

3. With a rolling pin, roll dough out very thin on a board.

4. Cut dough into shapes such as diamonds, hearts or fingers, or form into little rolls.

5. Heat oil to 190°C (375°F) and deep fry cheese bits until crisp and golden in color. Drain on paper toweling and serve.

Makes about 25 to 40 cheese bits

Mushrooms Parmesan

FUNGHI ALLA PARMIGIANA

1	kg	fresh mushrooms	2 pounds
60	mL	olive oil	4 tablespoons
30	mL	fresh chopped parsley	2 tablespoons
2		garlic cloves, finely chopped	
		Pinch of oregano	
250	mL	bread crumbs	1 cup
250	mL	grated Parmesan cheese	1 cup
		Salt and freshly ground pepper	
50	mL	hot water OR wine (optional)	¼ cup

1. Preheat oven to 180°C (350°F).

2. Clean mushrooms and place in a baking dish that has been brushed with a little olive oil.

3. Sprinkle mushrooms with parsley, garlic, oregano, half the bread crumbs and all the grated cheese. Add salt and pepper to taste.

4. Drizzle remaining oil over the mushrooms. Sprinkle with remaining bread crumbs.

5. Bake until mushrooms are tender (about 30 minutes). If mushrooms become too dry, add hot water or wine and bake an additional 5 minutes.

Makes 4 to 6 servings

Parmesan Fingers
CROSTINI ALLA PARMIGIANA

These cheese fingers are a delicious snack with wine or beer.

**Stale white bread, trimmed of crust
and cut lengthwise into quarters
Milk
Salt and freshly ground pepper
Grated Parmesan cheese
Oil for frying**

1. Soak as many bread fingers as required in milk to cover for 15 minutes.

2. Season with salt and pepper to taste and sprinkle generously with grated Parmesan cheese. Pat cheese into the bread with a wooden spoon.

3. Heat oil to 190°C (375°F) and fry bread fingers until crisp and golden brown.

Florentine Toast
CROSTINI ALLA FIORONTINA

This can be served as a light luncheon dish with salad. It takes only a few minutes to prepare and tastes delicious.

45	mL	sweet butter	3 tablespoons
1		medium-sized onion, chopped	
250	mL	sliced chicken livers	1 cup
50	mL	fresh chopped parsley	¼ cup

3		anchovy fillets, each chopped into 3 pieces	
125	mL	dry white wine	½ cup
125	mL	light cream OR sour cream	½ cup
		Salt and freshly ground pepper	
		Pinch of paprika	
4		slices white toast OR rusks	

1. Sauté in butter over low heat the onion, chicken livers and parsley until onion is golden and livers are tender; stir frequently.

2. Add anchovies and white wine and continue stirring.

3. Thicken the sauce with cream or sour cream and stir constantly over low heat.

4. Season with salt and pepper to taste and paprika.

5. Cover slices of toast with chicken livers and sauce.

Makes 4 servings

Tuna or Sardine Balls
POLPETTINE DI TONNO (O SARDINE)

500	g	canned tuna OR boned sardines	1 pound
1		egg	
60	mL	bread crumbs	4 tablespoons
50	mL	grated Romano cheese	¼ cup
1		sprig fresh parsley, chopped	
50	mL	sultana raisins	¼ cup
50	mL	pine nuts	¼ cup
		Salt and freshly ground pepper	
15	mL	all-purpose flour	1 tablespoon
50–125	mL	olive oil	¼–½ cup
2		garlic cloves, crushed	
250	mL	tomato sauce (see page 102)	1 cup

1. In a large mixing bowl, mash fish to a pulp with a wooden spoon. Add egg, bread crumbs, cheese, parsley, raisins, pine nuts and salt and pepper to taste. Mix well and shape into walnut-sized balls.

2. Heat oil to 190°C (375°F). Roll balls in flour and fry in oil until golden brown (about 10 minutes). Drain on paper toweling.

3. Add crushed garlic to the tomato sauce and heat. Add fish balls and cook for 10 minutes on low heat.

Makes 4 servings

FIRST COURSE

In a full-course Italian meal, the first course is usually served in two parts. First the soup, then the pasta, rice or polenta. Generally speaking, there are two kinds of soups: the *minestra*, which contains pasta, rice or potatoes; and *zuppa*, or broth (clear or thickened). The pasta, rice or polenta are usually served in small portions, especially if there is a large second course to follow. (Traditionally pasta is more commonly served in southern Italy, while polenta and rice are popular in the north).

SOUP

Jellied Veal Soup
BRODO DI VITELLO RISTRETTO

500	g	veal knuckles	1 pound
1	L	cold water	1 quart
1		small onion	
5	mL	salt	1 teaspoon
		Rind of ¼ lemon	
3		peppercorns	
4		sprigs fresh parsley	

1. Place all ingredients in a large saucepan or soup pot and slowly bring to a boil. Cover and simmer 3 to 5 hours.

2. Strain mixture and allow to cool. Cover and place in refrigerator overnight.

3. Remove surface fat.

4. Cut jelly with a knife or mash with a fork and serve in soup cups. Serve with garlic bread and salad.

Makes 4 servings

> *An antipasti plate* of devilled eggs, marinated artichoke hearts, olives and pecorino cheese. (Page 13).

Egg and Marsala Soup
GINESTRATA

Serve with a loaf of Italian bread and a bottle of wine on a cold winter day.

6		egg yolks	
125	mL	dry Marsala wine	½ cup
750	mL	chicken broth	3 cups
		Pinch of cinnamon	
		OR a 2.5-cm cinnamon stick	1-inch
60	mL	melted sweet butter	4 tablespoons
		Pinch of sugar	
		Dash of nutmeg	

1. Beat egg yolks in a large bowl. Gradually add wine, chicken broth and cinnamon, stirring constantly.

2. Place mixture in the top of a double boiler over simmering water. Slowly whisk in melted butter. When soup starts to thicken, remove from heat.

3. Preheat individual soup bowls. Combine sugar and nutmeg and sprinkle over soup before serving.

Makes 3 to 4 servings

Fish Soup with Noodles
ZUPPA DI PESCE CON TAGLIARINI

1.25	kg	whiting OR cod	2½ pounds
		OR Boston bluefish	
30	mL	butter	2 tablespoons
30	mL	olive oil	2 tablespoons
1		large onion, chopped	
1		large carrot, chopped	
3		stalks of celery, chopped	
2		large fresh tomatoes, peeled and chopped	
		Salt and freshly ground pepper	
2	L	boiling water	2 quarts
125	g	tagliarini pasta	¼ pound
		Grated Parmesan cheese	

Lettuce soup before bread is added. (Page 24).

1. Clean fish and leave whole.

2. Heat butter and olive oil in a large soup pot and sauté onion, carrot and celery over medium heat for 10 minutes. Add tomatoes, salt and pepper to taste and rapidly boiling water. Cover, reduce heat and simmer for 30 minutes.

3. Add fish. Bring to a boil, cover and reduce heat; simmer for 15 minutes. Remove fish. (Serve after soup course or at another meal.)

4. Strain broth. Return to pot, bring to a boil and add tagliarini. Cook uncovered until pasta is tender (about 15 minutes). Serve soup hot with grated Parmesan cheese.

Makes 6 servings

Lettuce Soup
MINESTRA DI LATTUGA

3		heads iceberg lettuce	
4		slices ham (any kind)	
1		onion, sliced	
1		carrot, sliced	
1		bay leaf	
2		whole cloves	
		Dash of thyme	
		Salt and freshly ground pepper	
2	L	boiling beef broth	2 quarts
1		loaf Italian bread	

1. Keeping the heads intact, clean lettuce and blanch in boiling salted water for 1 minute.

2. In a large soup pot, place ham slices, onion slices, carrot slices, bay leaf and cloves. Season with thyme and salt and pepper to taste.

3. Carefully place lettuce heads on top.

4. Gradually add broth, cover and simmer for 15 minutes. Remove lettuce and cut heads in half lengthwise.

5. Cut loaf of bread in half lengthwise and place lettuce halves on top of each half. Cut in slices 5 to 8-cm (2 to 3-inches) thick.

6. Arrange lettuce-covered bread slices in a soup tureen. Cover with hot soup and serve.

Makes 4 to 6 servings

Rice and Pea Soup
RISI E BISI

This soup is traditionally served on April 25, the Feast of St. Mark the Evangelist, Patron Saint of Venice. Peas and rice symbolize the return of spring.

90	mL	sweet butter	6 tablespoons
175	g	lean ham, chopped	6 ounces
1		medium-sized cooking onion, chopped	
15	mL	fresh chopped parsley	1 tablespoon
375	mL	uncooked long-grain rice	1½ cups
125	mL	dry white wine	½ cup
500	mL	shelled fresh small peas OR canned baby peas	2 cups
1.5	L	chicken broth	6 cups
7	mL	salt	1½ teaspoons
		Pinch of freshly ground pepper	
250	mL	freshly grated Parmesan cheese	1 cup

1. Melt 60 mL (4 tablespoons) of butter in a heavy saucepan. Add chopped ham, onion and parsley and cook 5 minutes over very low heat, stirring constantly. Add rice and cook until brown, stirring constantly (about 5 minutes).

2. Add wine and stir over low heat for about 2 minutes. Add peas, 500 mL (2 cups) of the broth and salt and pepper. Cover and bring to a boil; reduce heat to low and cook until broth is absorbed, stirring occasionally.

3. Add 250 mL (1 cup) more broth. When this is absorbed, add remaining broth and cook covered until rice and peas are tender.

4. Stir in Parmesan cheese, remaining butter and serve immediately.

Makes 6 servings

Royal Egg Soup
ZUPPA PAVESE

In 1525, King Frances I of France was defeated by Emperor Charles V, ruler of the Holy Roman Empire. Fleeing the battlefield in Pavese, Frances I stumbled around the countryside seeking refuge. He finally chanced upon a woman cooking soup and asked if he might have something to eat. The woman, realizing who he was, quickly ran to the hen house, fetched two eggs, and broke them onto a piece of bread in the soup bowl. From such humble beginnings, the recipe now has many sophisticated variations. Here's one of my favorites.

90	mL	sweet butter	6 tablespoons
30	mL	olive oil	2 tablespoons
6		thin slices of Italian bread, quartered	
1.5	L	chicken broth	6 cups
6		eggs	
		Freshly ground pepper	
300	mL	freshly grated Parmesan cheese	1¼ cups

1. Heat butter and oil in a frying pan and fry bread pieces on both sides until crisp and golden. Remove, drain on paper toweling and keep hot.

2. In a saucepan, bring broth to a boil. Break one egg into a shallow dish or saucer and slide it carefully into the broth. When egg is cooked, remove with slotted spoon to a heated soup tureen. Repeat with remaining 5 eggs, one by one.

3. Strain broth through cheese cloth and pour over eggs. Arrange bread pieces around the eggs. Sprinkle with pepper to taste and grated Parmesan cheese.

Makes 6 servings

Mushroom Soup, Piedmont Style
ZUPPA DI FUNGHI

75	mL	sweet butter	5 tablespoons
1	kg	fresh mushrooms, finely chopped	2 pounds
125	mL	dry Marsala wine	½ cup
125	mL	fresh chopped parsley	½ cup
2–3	mL	salt	½ teaspoon
		Pinch of freshly ground white pepper	
		Dash of freshly grated nutmeg	
1	L	béchamel sauce (see page 102)	4 cups
500	mL	chicken broth	2 cups
125	mL	light cream, at room temperature	½ cup

1. Heat butter in a large saucepan. Add mushrooms and sauté over very low heat 4 to 5 minutes.

2. Stir in wine, parsley, salt, white pepper and nutmeg.

26

3. Cook, stirring constantly, for 2 minutes over moderate heat. Remove from heat and stir in béchamel sauce.

4. Add chicken broth and bring to a boil over moderate heat, stirring constantly.

5. When soup starts to thicken, remove from heat. Slowly stir in cream and serve immediately.

Makes 6 to 8 servings

PASTA AND PASTA DISHES

Spaghettini, Bagarian Style
SPAGHETTINI ALLA BAGARIOTA

Pecorino is the generic name for all Italian ewe's milk cheeses. The original and best of all is Romano, a staple in every Italian kitchen.

2		garlic cloves, crushed	
60	mL	olive oil	4 tablespoons
1		can (800 mL) plum tomatoes	(28 ounces)
		Salt and freshly ground pepper	
1	L	pitted green olives, coarsely chopped	4 cups
2		leaves sweet basil, chopped	
1		small eggplant, diced	
500	g	spaghettini	1 pound
125	mL	grated Romano cheese	½ cup
15	mL	capers, rinsed in water	1 tablespoon

1. In a large saucepan, sauté garlic in oil until brown. Discard garlic.

2. Stir in tomatoes and salt and pepper to taste.

3. Add olives and basil; simmer uncovered about 45 minutes. Add eggplant and simmer until eggplant is tender (another 10 to 15 minutes).

4. Cook spaghettini in a large pot of boiling salted water until desired tenderness. Drain and arrange on a large platter.

5. Pour hot tomato sauce over pasta and toss. Sprinkle with grated cheese and capers and toss again. Serve immediately.

Makes 4 servings

Bolognese Lasagne

LASAGNE ALLA BOLOGNESE

500	g	lasagne noodles	1 pound
625	mL	Bolognese sauce	2½ cups
		(see recipe, page 100)	
500	mL	béchamel sauce	2 cups
		(see recipe, page 102)	
½–1	L	grated mozzarella cheese	2–4 cups
		Grated Parmesan cheese	

1. Preheat oven to 180°C (350°F). Boil lasagne in rapidly boiling salted water until tender but firm. Drain. Pour 1 L (4 cups) of cold water over noodles to cool and drain well.

2. In a large rectangular baking dish or lasagne pan, layer ingredients in the following sequence: Bolognese sauce, béchamel sauce, mozzarella cheese and lasagne noodles. Repeat. Top with a layer of mozzarella cheese.

3. Bake 20 to 30 minutes or until top is bubbly (not dried out).

4. Serve hot with grated Parmesan cheese.

Makes 6 servings

Homemade Pasta

PASTA FATTA IN CASA

After eating homemade pasta, you may never go back to the packaged variety. Pasta dough can be cut into hundreds of different shapes and sizes, including fettuccine, tagliatelle, cannelloni, tortellini, ravioli and lasagne.

175	mL	all-purpose flour	¾ cup
1		egg	
1		egg white	
15	mL	olive oil	1 tablespoon
		Pinch of salt	
		Few drops of water OR beaten egg	
		OR sherry	

1. Form a mound of flour on a pastry board. Into the center break an egg, then add the egg white, oil and salt.

2. Gather up the flour and knead, adding a little water if the dough feels too dry. (You can also use a food processor or mixer with a dough hook for kneading; follow manufacturer's directions.) Knead until dough forms into a smooth elastic ball (about 10 minutes).

3. Wrap dough in tin foil or waxed paper and let stand for 10 minutes.

4. Divide dough into 2 balls and place one at a time on a floured surface. Press with hands to form an oblong shape about 5-cm (2-inches) thick. Dust with flour.

5. Unless you're using a pasta machine to roll out dough, use a heavy rolling pin. Roll away from yourself, and after each roll, turn dough 90 degrees, or a quarter of a circle. Repeat rolling and turning until dough is paper thin.

6. Cut dough with a sharp knife or use a pasta machine to make whatever size or shape you wish. Pasta may be refrigerated in a tightly sealed plastic bag for up to 24 hours before cooking.

Makes 4 to 6 servings

Spaghetti with Anchovies
SPAGHETTI ALLE ACCIUGHE

125	mL	olive oil	½ cup
1		garlic clove, crushed	
12		anchovy fillets, cut into	
		1-cm pieces	½-inch
		Freshly ground pepper	
500	g	spaghetti	1 pound
250	mL	grated Parmesan cheese	1 cup
15	mL	fresh chopped parsley	1 tablespoon

1. Heat oil in a frying pan. Sauté garlic until golden brown and discard.

2. Fry anchovies in oil for 2 minutes, stirring constantly. Add a little pepper.

3. In a large pot of boiling salted water, cook spaghetti to desired tenderness and drain.

4. Arrange spaghetti on individual heated plates.

5. Pour anchovies over the spaghetti and top with grated Parmesan cheese and fresh chopped parsley. Serve immediately.

Makes 4 to 6 servings

Pasta with Clam Sauce

PASTA AI VONGOLI

12		littleneck clams	
		OR 1 can (140 g) clams	(5 ounces)
2		garlic cloves, finely chopped	
60	mL	olive oil	4 tablespoons
1		can (800 mL) plum tomatoes, drained	(28 ounces)
15	mL	fresh chopped OR dried parsley	1 tablespoon
		Salt and freshly ground pepper	
500	g	pasta (spaghetti, linguine or any other type)	1 pound
		Grated Parmesan cheese (optional)	

1. If using fresh clams, scrub clam shells and rinse in cold water until all sand is removed. Insert a thin knife blade and pry shells open. Reserve both clams and juice.

2. Cut clams into small pieces and place in a bowl with their juice.

3. Sauté garlic in hot oil in a saucepan. Add clam juice, drained tomatoes, chopped parsley, salt and pepper to taste; simmer slowly, uncovered, for 40 minutes.

4. Add the clams and raise heat; cook for 2 minutes. (Prolonged cooking toughens clams.) If using canned clams, do not increase heat; allow clams and sauce to simmer slowly for 5 minutes.

5. Cook the pasta in a large pot of boiling salted water until desired tenderness. Drain and place on a large platter. Pour sauce on top and toss. Serve hot with grated Parmesan cheese.

Makes 4 servings

Original Lasagne

LASAGNE ORIGINALE

This dish is the forerunner of modern lasagne. The tomato sauce is a comparatively recent addition, however, since tomatoes were introduced to Italy only 400 years ago. Be sure to use the best quality mafalda, a thin lasagne with curly ends.

500	g	mafalda pasta	1 pound
½–1	kg	ricotta cheese	1–2 pounds
125	mL	grated cacciocavallo cheese	½ cup
375	mL	tomato sauce (see recipe, page 102)	1½ cups
15	mL	brandy (optional)	1 tablespoon
125	mL	dry white wine OR vermouth (optional)	½ cup
		Grated Parmesan cheese	

1. Preheat oven to 180°C (350°F).

2. Cook mafalda in a large pot of boiling salted water according to package instructions or until tender but firm. Drain. Remove to a bowl of ice water and set aside.

3. Whirl ricotta in a blender or beat with an electric mixer until smooth and light.

4. In a greased lasagne pan or large rectangular baking dish, arrange alternate layers of pasta and ricotta cheese, starting and finishing with pasta. Top with grated cacciocavallo.

5. In a small saucepan, heat tomato sauce with brandy and white wine; pour over lasagne. Bake until hot (15 to 20 minutes). Serve with grated Parmesan cheese.

Makes 4 to 6 servings

Noodles and Tuna
TAGLIATELLE AL TONNO

1		can (184 g) tuna, packed in oil	(6½ ounces)
30	mL	grated Romano cheese	2 tablespoons
15	mL	fresh chopped parsley	1 tablespoon
500	g	tagliatelle noodles	1 pound
2		eggs, beaten	

1. Combine tuna, cheese, parsley and mix well. Set aside.

2. Cook noodles in a large pot of salted boiling water to desired tenderness. Drain well. Remove to a large serving bowl.

3. Add eggs to noodles and toss. Add tuna mixture and toss again. Let stand a few minutes before serving.

Makes 4 to 6 servings

Spaghetti with Meat Sauce

SPAGHETTI CON CARNE

		Butter and oil for frying	
225	g	ground beef	½ pound
2		garlic cloves, chopped	
45	mL	dried mushrooms, soaked in warm water and squeezed dry	3 tablespoons
1		onion, chopped	
1		small carrot, chopped	
1		small parsnip, chopped	
1		stick celery, chopped	
1		small turnip, chopped (optional)	
250	mL	boiling beef broth	1 cup
1		can (150 mL) tomato paste	(5½ ounces)
		Salt and freshly ground pepper	
1		sprig each thyme and parsley	
500	g	spaghetti	1 pound
		Grated Parmesan cheese	

1. Heat equal parts of butter and oil and sauté meat for a few minutes, until brown. Add garlic, mushrooms and vegetables and brown them slightly.

2. Cover with beef broth and stir in tomato paste, salt and pepper to taste, thyme and parsley. Cover and simmer gently for 2 hours, stirring frequently.

3. Cook spaghetti in rapidly boiling salted water to desired tenderness. Drain.

4. Place spaghetti in a large serving bowl. Cover with meat sauce and toss. Sprinkle with grated Parmesan cheese and toss again. Serve immediately.

Makes 4 servings

Homemade Egg Noodles

PASTA ALL'UOVO FATTA IN CASA

This technique takes time and practice, but it's worth it. These noodles are heavenly.

1.7	L	all-purpose flour	7 cups
		Pinch of salt	
8		eggs	
60	mL	heavy cream OR sherry	4 tablespoons
500	g	fresh spinach, cooked, passed through a sieve and thoroughly dried (optional)	1 pound

1. Sift flour with a good pinch of salt onto a pastry board. Make a hollow in the center and break the eggs into it. Add cream or sherry.

2. Using your hand or a wooden fork, blend the flour into the eggs, gradually adding a little more flour until all is used up.

3. Knead as you would bread, until the dough holds together and becomes flexible (about 15 to 20 minutes). (Or use a food processor or mixer with dough hook, according to directions.) Allow dough to stand for 30 minutes in a bowl covered with a damp tea towel.

4. Divide dough into 6 pieces and shape into balls. Roll each out to paper thinness, about the size of a large pizza. Allow to dry for 15 to 20 minutes.

5. Fold loosely and cut into strips using a very sharp knife. The width will depend on their eventual use: narrow for soup noodles, wide for lasagne and medium for most other uses. Hang the strips on a tea towel over the back of a chair away from the heat; allow to dry (about 20 minutes). Don't leave too long or they may become brittle. Noodles may be used immediately or stored in a dry place for future use.

Note: To make green noodles, omit the cream or sherry and add just enough spinach to give dough a pale green color. Allow slightly longer to dry.

Makes 6 to 8 servings

Noodles and Asparagus
TAGLIARINI E ASPARAGI

1	kg	fresh asparagus	2 pounds
2		garlic cloves, crushed	
60	mL	olive oil	4 tablespoons
1		can (800 g) plum tomatoes	(28 ounces)
		Salt and freshly ground pepper	
500	g	tagliarini pasta	1 pound
125	mL	grated Parmesan OR Romano cheese	½ cup

1. Clean asparagus and remove any tough ends. Cut stalks in half.

2. In a large saucepan, sauté garlic and asparagus in olive oil for 10 minutes over low heat. Remove garlic.

3. Add tomatoes and salt and pepper to taste. Bring to a boil, cover and reduce heat; simmer covered for 30 minutes, stirring occasionally to prevent burning.

4. Cook tagliarini in a large pot of boiling salted water until desired tenderness. Drain.

5. Place pasta on a warm serving platter. Cover with asparagus and tomato sauce and toss. Sprinkle with grated cheese and toss again. Serve hot.

Makes 4 servings

Fusilli with Cauliflower
FUSILLI E CAVOLFIORI

This is a variation of a 2,000-year-old recipe – just as good today as it was then.

1		small cauliflower	
60	mL	olive oil	4 tablespoons
1		large onion, diced	
3		anchovy fillets, cut in small pieces	
500	g	plum tomatoes, peeled and chopped	1 pound
15	mL	pine nuts	1 tablespoon
15	mL	currants	1 tablespoon
		Salt and freshly ground pepper	
500	g	fusilli pasta	1 pound
		Grated Romano cheese (optional)	

1. Remove leaves from cauliflower. Wash well and separate into small flowerets. Cook in rapidly boiling water until tender, but not soft. Drain and set aside.

2. Heat oil in a saucepan. Cook onion for about 3 minutes or until soft. Add anchovies and stir until they dissolve (about 2 minutes). Add tomatoes, cover and simmer for about 20 minutes.

3. Add cauliflower, pine nuts and currants. Add a pinch of salt and pepper to taste. Mix well and keep hot over low heat.

4. Cook fusilli in a large pot of rapidly boiling salted water to desired tenderness. Drain.

5. Place pasta in a large serving bowl. Add cauliflower and sauce. Toss and serve hot. If you like, sprinkle grated Romano cheese on top before serving.

Makes 4 to 6 servings

Conchiglie Seafood Salad
INSALATA DI FRUTTI DI MARE

For as long as there has been pasta, there have been pasta leftovers. In Roman times, the shepherds packed their "lunch boxes" with cold pasta leftovers and fruit. Travelers carried it with them for refreshment on their journeys. Today we no longer need leftovers as an excuse for serving cold pasta. Mixed with chicken or fish, vegetables and mayonnaise, it makes a wonderful lunch or dinner salad. Here's my favorite recipe for cold pasta (or pasta fredda).

500	g	conchiglie (shell) pasta	1 pound
125	mL	mayonnaise	½ cup
1		can (184 g) tuna fish	(6½ ounces)
		OR 250 mL diced cooked chicken breast	1 cup
1		can (142 g) clams, drained	(5 ounces)
		OR 250 mL cooked softshell clams (shells removed)	1 cup
1		can (142 g) shrimp, diced	(5 ounces)
		OR 250 mL fresh shrimp, cooked, shelled, deveined and diced	1 cup
1		can (300 mL) baby peas, drained	(10 ounces)
		Pinch of freshly ground pepper	
		Pinch of paprika	
		Dash of cognac OR vermouth	

1. Cook pasta in a large pot of boiling salted water until desired tenderness. Drain. Rinse with ice cold water and drain again.

2. In a large bowl, combine pasta with remaining ingredients. Toss and chill for 2 to 3 hours. Serve cold on lettuce garnished with hard-cooked eggs, halved, and parsley sprigs. Serve with green salad and Italian bread.

Makes 6 to 8 servings

Variation: For an antipasto, omit the green peas and serve on clam shells.

Spaghetti with Eggs and Pancetta
SPAGHETTI ALLA CARBONARA

This is one of the oldest known pasta dishes. The scrumptious sauce is made with eggs, bacon and onions.

250	g	pancetta OR back bacon, cut into 1.5-cm pieces	½ pound ½-inch
125	mL	chopped onion	½ cup
125	mL	oil OR butter	½ cup
3		eggs, beaten	
125	mL	grated Parmesan cheese	½ cup
30	mL	finely chopped parsley (optional)	2 tablespoons
		Pinch of freshly ground pepper	
500	g	spaghetti OR spaghettini	1 pound
		Grated Parmesan cheese	

1. Sauté bacon and onion in oil until bacon is slightly crisp and onion is tender.

2. In a mixing bowl, combine eggs, grated cheese, parsley and pepper.

3. Cook spaghetti in a large pot of boiling salted water until desired tenderness. Drain and place in a large serving bowl. Do not allow to cool.

4. Stir in egg mixture and toss; add bacon mixture and toss again. Sprinkle with lots of grated Parmesan cheese and serve hot with salad.

Makes 4 servings

RICE AND POLENTA

Rice Croquettes
CROCCHETTE DI RISO

500	mL	rice	2 cups
2		eggs, beaten	
125	mL	grated Parmesan cheese	½ cup
30	mL	fresh chopped parsley	2 tablespoons
		Salt and freshly ground pepper	
250	mL	toasted bread crumbs	1 cup
500	mL	peanut oil	2 cups

1. Cook rice in water according to package directions until soft. Cool to room temperature.

2. Add eggs to rice and mix. Stir in cheese, parsley, salt and pepper to taste; mix thoroughly.

3. Roll into small balls (the size of golf balls) and roll in bread crumbs.

4. Deep fry in oil heated to 190°C (375°F) until golden brown (about 3 minutes). Serve as a side dish with meat or fowl.

Makes 6 to 8 servings

Polenta with Sausage
POLENTA ALLA SALSICCIA

500	mL	polenta	2 cups
		Cold water	
1.5	L	salted boiling water	6 cups
500	g	Italian sausage, cut into small pieces	1 pound
10	mL	olive oil	2 teaspoons
1		garlic clove, finely chopped	
30	mL	fresh chopped parsley	2 tablespoons
500	mL	fresh plum tomatoes, peeled OR canned, drained tomatoes	2 cups
30	mL	butter	2 tablespoons
		Salt and freshly ground pepper	
125	mL	grated Parmesan cheese	½ cup

1. Combine polenta with just enough cold water to give it a runny consistency. Add to rapidly boiling salted water in a saucepan, stirring constantly to prevent lumping, and reduce heat to low. Cover and cook 30 minutes, stirring frequently so polenta doesn't stick. Remove from heat.

2. Fry sausage in oil for about 15 minutes. Stir in garlic, parsley, tomatoes, butter and salt and pepper to taste; cover and cook over low heat about 1 hour.

3. Reheat polenta for a few minutes, stirring frequently, until hot. Spread half the hot polenta on a warm serving platter. Cover with half the sausage mixture. Place remaining polenta on top, then remaining sausage mixture. Sprinkle with grated Parmesan cheese and serve.

Makes 6 to 8 servings

Polenta and Mushroom Pie
POLENTA E FUNGHI IN CASSERUOLA

500	g	polenta	1 pound
2	L	boiling water	2 quarts
10	mL	salt	2 teaspoons
750	mL	mushroom sauce (see below)	3 cups
125	mL	butter	½ cup
		Salt and freshly ground pepper	
60	mL	grated Parmesan OR Romano cheese	4 tablespoons

1. Cook polenta in boiling salted water until thick (see note on page 10).

2. Place in a greased 2-L (9 × 5 × 3-inch) loaf pan and allow to set for about 2 hours. (If not used immediately, store covered in refrigerator after it sets.)

3. Slice "loaf" of polenta lengthwise into 3 layers, about 2-cm (1-inch) thick.

4. Preheat oven to 180°C (350°F).

5. In a greased 4-L (9 × 13-inch) rectangular casserole, place a layer of sliced polenta. Cover with 250 mL (1 cup) of mushroom sauce and top with slivers of butter and salt and pepper to taste. Repeat two more times, ending with sauce.

6. Sprinkle with grated cheese and bake for 45 minutes. If desired, serve with extra cheese and sauce.

Makes 6 servings

Mushroom Sauce
SALSA DI FUNGHI

250	mL	dried Italian mushrooms	1 cup
		OR 500 g fresh mushrooms, sliced	1 pound
1		garlic clove, finely chopped	
15	mL	olive oil	1 tablespoon
15	mL	fresh chopped parsley	1 tablespoon
500	mL	béchamel sauce (see recipe, page 102), warmed	2 cups

1. If using dried mushrooms, soak in about 125 mL (½ cup) water until all the moisture is absorbed. Dry and slice.

2. In a saucepan, brown garlic in oil and sauté mushrooms and parsley about 3 minutes over low heat.

3. Drain off any excess oil and stir in warmed béchamel sauce. Blend well.

Makes about 750 mL (3 cups)

Rice with Shrimp
RISO CON GAMBERETTI (O SCAMPI)

1	kg	raw shrimp in the shell	2 pounds
250	mL	butter	1 cup
1		onion, sliced	
1		carrot, finely chopped	
15	mL	fresh chopped parsley	1 tablespoon
		Pinch of thyme	
1		bay leaf	
30	mL	cognac	2 tablespoons
½		onion, finely chopped	
15	mL	olive oil	1 tablespoon
625	mL	uncooked long-grain rice	2½ cups
250	mL	dry red wine	1 cup

1. Shell and devein shrimp. Reserve shells.

2. Heat shrimp shells in cold salted water and boil, covered, for 25 minutes; reserve 1 litre (1 quart) of this stock.

3. Heat half the butter in a large saucepan and sauté shrimp, sliced onion, carrot, parsley, thyme and bay leaf until onion is golden brown.

4. Add cognac and cook until it has evaporated.

5. In a separate saucepan, sauté the finely chopped onion in oil and remaining butter. Add the rice and cook until golden (about 5 minutes). Do not let it burn.

6. Add wine to the rice, and cook until it evaporates.

7. Add the litre (quart) of stock from the shrimp shells and cook uncovered until rice is tender and moisture is absorbed (about 20 minutes).

8. Remove rice to a large serving platter. Pour shrimps and sauce on top and serve immediately.

Makes 4 to 6 servings

Saffron Rice
RISOTTO ALLA MILANESE (ZAFFERANO)

Saffron was used by the very rich during the Renaissance because of its gilded look. Not only because so much importance was placed on appearance, but because alchemists believed that gold was good for the heart. This tradition is now lost in most of Italy, but Lombardy still uses saffron in many of its distinctive dishes, like this one.

250	mL	sweet butter	1 cup
1		onion, chopped	
		Freshly ground white pepper	
500	mL	dry white wine	2 cups
625	mL	long-grain rice	2½ cups
		Salt	
3	mL	crushed saffron	½ teaspoon
625–875	mL	chicken broth	2½–3½ cups
500	mL	grated Parmesan cheese	2 cups

1. Melt two-thirds of the butter in a heavy frying pan. Add the onion and white pepper and cook over low heat until onion is golden.

2. Add wine and raise heat to moderate; reduce wine by half.

3. Add the rice and salt to taste and cook for 2 to 3 minutes, stirring constantly until wine is absorbed. Add saffron and 500 mL (2 cups) of chicken broth and cook until broth is absorbed, stirring constantly.

4. Add remaining chicken broth, a little at a time, waiting each time until broth has evaporated before adding more. Use only as much broth as needed to make rice tender, but firm. Stir occasionally so rice won't stick to pan.

5. Stir in remaining butter and grated cheese and remove from heat. Serve hot. If desired, serve with extra grated Parmesan cheese.

Makes 4 to 6 servings

Note: This dish requires constant attention or the rice can stick and burn.

Pasta assortment: (1) tagliarini, (2) conchiglie or gnocchi pasta, (3) fusilli, (4) spaghetti, (5) mafalda and (6) macaroni elbows. (Pages 27–35).

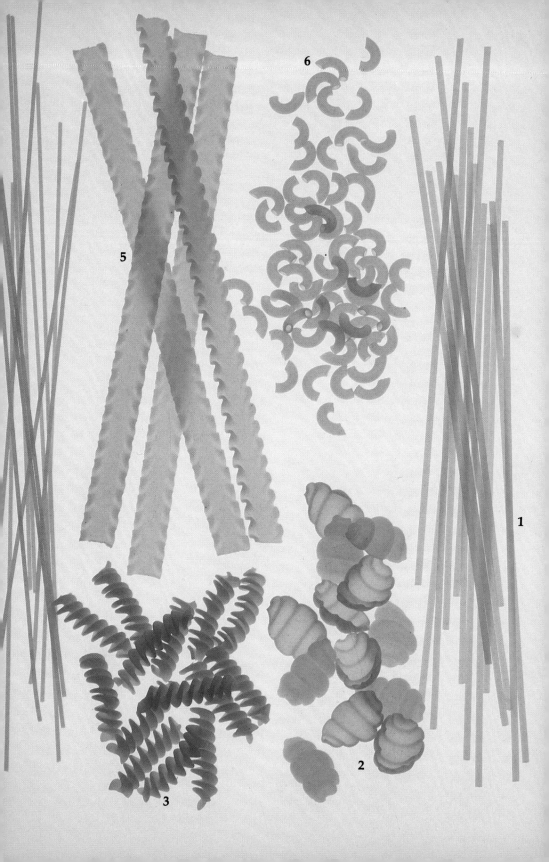

SECOND COURSE

Fish, meat or fowl comprise the second course of an Italian meal. For full-course dinners, there's often two parts to this course: fish first, then meat or fowl.

Fish dominates the table in Italy, a land with a large southern seacoast and numerous rivers in the north. Red mullet and eels are particular favorites.

Because meat is scarce and costly, it has had a limited place in the diet. Moreover, in strict Roman Catholic homes, there are myriad holidays requiring that meatless meals be eaten.

Historically Italians are big pork eaters. But when available, veal is the most highly preferred meat. True veal is four to 14-week-old cattle fed on a special diet of dried milk and eggs.

Game at one time was part of the daily diet. Medieval Italian nobility kept game reserves for sport and a ready supply of hare, deer and pheasant. But today, while game is still popular in Italy, it's far less prevalent in the diet. Of the domesticated birds, chicken is the most popular.

Also part of the second course are the accompanying vegetables, including such notables as eggplant, zucchini and fennel. In addition to the sumptuous meat, fish and fowl recipes in this section, there's a selection of tasty vegetable dishes.

Polenta with sausage served decoratively on a platter. (Page 37).

FISH AND SEAFOOD

Home-Style Fillet of Bass
PESCE PERSICO

2	L	water	2 quarts
15	mL	salt	1 tablespoon
1		bay leaf	
15	mL	wine vinegar	1 tablespoon
		Pinch of thyme	
1	kg	bass fillets	2 pounds
60	mL	heavy cream	4 tablespoons
45	mL	melted butter	3 tablespoons
250	mL	béchamel sauce (see page 102)	1 cup
4		hard-cooked eggs, chopped	
125	mL	finely chopped parsley	½ cup

1. Heat water to which salt, bay leaf, vinegar and thyme have been added and boil for 5 minutes.

2. Add the fillets. Cover and cook over low heat about 10 minutes.

3. In a separate pan over low heat, add cream and butter to the béchamel sauce and mix well.

4. Drain fillets and place them on a serving dish.

5. Pour white sauce on top and sprinkle with eggs and fresh parsley. Serve hot.

Makes 4 to 6 servings

Broiled Lobster Tails with Vermouth
CODA DI ARAGOSTA AL VERMOUTH

This dish was created by a cook of the beautiful Contessa Castiglione, one of the most famous mistresses of Napoleon III. The technique is very delicate, so give it your full concentration.

50	mL	finely chopped onion	¼ cup
500	mL	dry white vermouth	2 cups
250	mL	sweet red vermouth	1 cup
		OR Marsala wine	
500	mL	heavy cream	2 cups

4		egg yolks	
5	mL	salt	1 teaspoon
2–3	mL	freshly ground pepper	½ teaspoon
1–2	mL	cayenne pepper	¼ teaspoon
125	mL	sweet butter	½ cup
4		lobster tails (each 175 g)	(each 6 ounces)
125	mL	olive oil	½ cup
2		lemons, cut into wedges	

1. Preheat broiler to 240°C (475°F).

2. Place onion and white and red vermouths in a saucepan. Bring to a boil and cook over high heat until vermouths are almost evaporated.

3. In another saucepan, simmer cream until it is reduced by two-thirds. (This takes great care. Do not stir; just move pan very gently back and forth on burner. Be very careful cream doesn't curdle.) When reduced, add 30 mL (2 tablespoons) of cream to the egg yolks and mix well. Then slowly add egg yolks to cream, stirring constantly.

4. Combine onion and vermouth mixture with cream and egg yolks. Season with salt, pepper and cayenne pepper. Cook over boiling water, adding butter a little at a time and beating constantly with a wire whisk until thickened. Taste for seasoning. Remove from heat and keep hot.

5. Wash lobster tails and split in half lengthwise. Season with salt and pepper, brush with oil and broil for about 25 minutes, turning and brushing with oil frequently. When done, place lobster on a heated serving platter surrounded with lemon wedges. Serve sauce separately in a gravy boat.

Makes 4 servings

Squid and Tomato

CALAMARI AL POMODORO

3		garlic cloves, crushed	
90	mL	olive oil	6 tablespoons
2	kg	squid, cleaned and cut into small pieces	4½ pounds
		Salt and freshly ground pepper	
		Pinch of oregano	
250	mL	dry sherry	1 cup
500	mL	drained canned tomatoes	2 cups
15	mL	fresh chopped parsley	1 tablespoon

1. In a large frying pan, sauté garlic in oil for 4 minutes. Discard garlic.

2. Add squid to oil, cover and fry for 10 minutes.

3. Season with salt and pepper to taste, oregano and sherry and cook, uncovered, over low heat for 15 minutes.

4. Add tomatoes and parsley and simmer, uncovered, until squid is tender (about 20 minutes more). Serve on rice, polenta or toast.

Makes 4 to 6 servings

Sole with Shrimps and Artichoke Hearts

SOGLIOLA, SCAMPI E CARCIOFINI

250	mL	olive oil	1 cup
50	mL	lemon juice	¼ cup
8	mL	salt	1¾ teaspoon
		Freshly ground white pepper	
1	kg	fillets of sole, cut in	2 pounds
		5 × 10 cm pieces	2 × 4 inch
6		large shrimp, shelled and deveined	
150	mL	sweet butter	⅔ cup
250	mL	chopped green onions	1 cup
3–4	mL	freshly ground black pepper	¾ teaspoon
125	mL	tomato sauce OR purée	½ cup
		(see recipes, pages 102 and 103)	
50	mL	dry vermouth	¼ cup
2		packages (each 250 g) frozen	(each 9 ounces)
		artichoke hearts, thawed	
125	mL	heavy cream	½ cup

1. In a large mixing bowl, combine olive oil, lemon juice, 3 mL (¾ teaspoons) salt and a sprinkle of white pepper to taste. Add the sole and shrimp and marinate one hour, turning occasionally. Remove sole and shrimp from marinade.

2. Grease a Dutch oven or large saucepan with 15 mL (1 tablespoon) of butter and add the shrimp, sole, green onions, 2 mL (½ teaspoon) black pepper, tomato sauce and vermouth. Bring to a boil and cook covered for 5 minutes.

3. Remove from heat. Remove the sole and shrimp, keeping them hot while preparing artichokes.

4. In a saucepan melt 60 mL (4 tablespoons) butter. Add artichokes, 5 mL (1 teaspoon) salt and 1–2 mL (¼ teaspoon) black pepper. Sauté for 8 minutes.

5. Reheat the tomato mixture in the Dutch oven and boil gently, uncovered, until thickened. Add heavy cream and cook over medium heat until mixture is reduced by one-third.

6. Remove from heat and stir in remaining butter.

7. Place artichoke hearts on a platter, cover with the warm sole and shrimp and top with tomato sauce. Serve with rice and parsley butter.

Makes 6 servings

Mullet, Livornese Style

TRIGLIE ALLA LIVORNESE

6		mullet	
		Salt and freshly ground pepper	
125	mL	all-purpose flour	½ cup
1		onion, chopped	
1		stalk of celery, chopped	
15	mL	fresh chopped parsley	1 tablespoon
125	mL	oil	½ cup
1	L	fresh tomatoes, peeled and chopped	4 cups
		OR drained canned tomatoes	
		Pinch of thyme	
2		bay leaves	

1. Clean the fish. Season with salt and pepper to taste and roll in flour.

2. In a large saucepan, sauté onion, celery and parsley in half the oil until onion is translucent. Add tomatoes, thyme and bay leaves and simmer uncovered until onion and celery are soft. Remove bay leaves.

3. Remove from heat and strain through a food mill or through a sieve. Return sauce to pan.

4. In a large frying pan, lightly brown fish in remaining oil.

5. Transfer fish to sauce and simmer gently, covered, until fish is cooked (about 15 minutes); do not overcook. Serve hot, garnished with sprigs of fresh parsley.

Makes 4 to 6 servings

Whiting, Genovese Style

MERLUZZO CON SALSA POMODORO

If whiting isn't available, substitute Boston bluefish, turbot or cod.

60	mL	butter	4 tablespoons
250	mL	red table wine	1 cup
2		bay leaves	
		Pinch of marjoram	
		Salt and freshly ground pepper	
500	g	whiting fish	1 pound
250	mL	tomato sauce (see recipe, page 102)	1 cup
30	mL	mayonnaise	2 tablespoons
30–45	mL	vegetable stock (optional)	2–3 tablespoons
125	g	fresh OR canned whole button mushrooms (if fresh, blanch 3–5 minutes in water and sauté in butter) (optional)	¼ pound

1. Heat butter and wine in a frying pan. Stir in bay leaves, marjoram and salt and pepper to taste.

2. Add fish and cook over high heat for a few minutes, turning fish over occasionally.

3. Remove bay leaves. Add tomato sauce, mayonnaise and vegetable stock. Stir gently until heated through and fish is cooked.

4. Remove fish to a serving platter and keep hot.

5. Add mushrooms to the sauce and heat for an additional minute or two. Pour sauce into a gravy boat and serve with fish.

Makes 2 to 4 servings

Savory Sole

SOGLIOLA IN SAPORE

This cold dish is terrific with cold pasta salads.

2		large sole (each 1.5–2 kg)	(each 3–4 pounds)
30	mL	all-purpose flour	2 tablespoons
		Salt and freshly ground pepper	
		Pinch of cinnamon	

45	mL	olive oil	3 tablespoons
3		onions, chopped	
30	mL	pine nuts	2 tablespoons
30	mL	raisins	2 tablespoons
250	mL	white wine vinegar	1 cup
		OR dry white wine left	
		uncovered overnight	

1. Wash and skin the fish, removing heads and fins, but do not fillet.

2. Combine flour, salt and pepper to taste and cinnamon and rub well into fish.

3. Heat the oil in a large frying pan and sauté onions until brown. Remove onions.

4. Place fish, pine nuts and raisins into same pan and fry the fish on both sides until done; fish should be golden brown in color. Remove with care and place in a deep bowl.

5. Return onions to the pan, add vinegar and bring to a boil. Remove from heat and allow to cool.

6. Pour mixture over fish and refrigerate for several hours. Serve chilled.

Makes 4 to 6 servings

Trout with Mushrooms
TROTA AI FUNGHI

750	mL	fresh mushrooms, preferably button	3 cups
6		cleaned trout, with heads and tails on	
		Salt and freshly ground pepper	
		All-purpose flour	
15	mL	oil	1 tablespoon
125	mL	butter	½ cup
3		green onions, finely chopped	
30	mL	fresh chopped parsley	2 tablespoons
		Juice of ½ lemon	
175	mL	bread crumbs	¾ cup

1. Wash mushrooms and slice thin. Set aside.

2. Season fish inside and out with salt and pepper to taste.

3. Roll fish in flour and fry gently in oil and half the butter until lightly browned (about 10 minutes on each side).

4. Fry onions and mushrooms in a separate pan with remaining butter until mushrooms soften (about 6 minutes). Add parsley, lemon juice and salt to taste. Toss lightly.

5. Arrange trout 2 cm (1 inch) apart on a large platter with mushroom mixture between.

6. In same oil trout was fried in, fry bread crumbs until crisp. Sprinkle over trout and mushrooms.

Makes 6 servings

POULTRY AND GAME

Grandma Agnese's Venison

CERVO ALLA NONNA AGNESE

1	L	wine vinegar	1 quart
2		large carrots	
2		garlic cloves, crushed	
30	mL	fresh chopped parsley	2 tablespoons
2		whole cloves	
2		large onions, quartered	
2	kg	venison	4 pounds
		Salt and freshly ground pepper	
45	mL	all-purpose flour	3 tablespoons
4		strips salt pork OR side bacon	
250	mL	sherry	1 cup

1. Pour wine vinegar into a large soup pot and bring to a boil. Remove from heat.

2. Add carrots, garlic, parsley, cloves and 1 onion, quartered. Allow to cool.

3. Place venison in mixture and marinate in refrigerator 24 hours; turn often.

4. Preheat oven to 200°C (400°F).

5. Remove venison from marinade and dry with paper toweling. (Reserve marinade.) Sprinkle with salt and pepper to taste. Dredge with flour.

6. Place venison in a shallow roasting pan. Put strips of salt pork over meat and place remaining onion in the pan.

7. Place meat in oven. Brown 15 minutes on one side, then turn and brown other side 15 minutes.

8. Remove vegetables and 125 mL (½ cup) of liquid from the marinade and place in roasting pan. Reduce heat to 180°C (350°F) and baste occasionally. Roast until tender (about 1½ hours). Remove venison from roasting pan.

9. To make gravy, add sherry to pan drippings and simmer gently on top of stove for about 10 minutes. Slice meat and serve with hot gravy.

Makes 6 to 8 servings

Note: If venison isn't available, substitute rabbit or pheasant.

Rabbit, Hunter's Style
CONIGLIO ALLA CACCIATORA

2.5	kg	rabbit, cleaned and cut into serving pieces	5 pounds
500	mL	Burgundy wine	2 cups
60	mL	olive oil	4 tablespoons
1		onion, chopped	
1		garlic clove, crushed	
500	mL	canned tomatoes	2 cups
		Salt and freshly ground pepper	
		Pinch of rosemary	

1. Marinate rabbit in Burgundy wine for at least 6 hours, preferably overnight, in the refrigerator.

2. Heat oil in a large saucepan and sauté chopped onion for about 3 minutes. Add rabbit (reserving marinade), garlic, tomatoes, salt and pepper to taste. Cover and simmer for 30 minutes.

3. Slowly add Burgundy marinade and rosemary. Cook covered until rabbit is tender (about 20 minutes). Remove garlic clove and serve.

Makes 4 to 6 servings

Chicken in Cream

POLLO ALLA CREMA

2		sweet onions, finely sliced	
50	mL	butter	¼ cup
2.5	kg	chicken pieces	5 pounds
5	mL	salt	1 teaspoon
		Freshly ground pepper	
125	mL	heavy cream	½ cup
250	mL	béchamel sauce (see recipe, page 102)	1 cup
15	mL	tomato paste	1 tablespoon
		Pinch of curry powder	
2–3	mL	paprika	½ teaspoon
		Juice of 1 lemon	
500	g	mushrooms, sliced	1 pound

1. In a large saucepan, sauté onions in butter for 2 minutes. Add chicken pieces, salt and pepper to taste and cover with cream. Simmer, covered, for 30 minutes, stirring occasionally.

2. Remove chicken pieces and set aside. Keep warm.

3. Add béchamel sauce and tomato paste to cream sauce and boil for 2 minutes, stirring constantly. Remove from heat and strain. Return to saucepan.

4. Add curry powder, paprika and lemon juice to sauce and blend well. Add cooked chicken and mushrooms. Simmer, uncovered, for 15 minutes. Serve with rice or boiled potatoes.

Makes 4 servings

Roast Turkey with Chestnut Stuffing

TACCHINO ARROSTO RIPIENO CON CASTAGNE

1	kg	Italian chestnuts, roasted and shelled	2 pounds
125	g	ground beef	¼ pound
60	g	ground veal OR pork	2 ounces
125	g	ground pork sausage	¼ pound
		Turkey liver and gizzard, finely chopped	

		Salt and freshly ground pepper	
90	g	prunes, soaked in water 1 hour, pitted and chopped	3 ounces
45	mL	olive oil	3 tablespoons
175	mL	grated Romano cheese	¾ cup
2		eggs, beaten	
375	mL	dry white wine	1½ cups
7	kg	turkey, trussed and ready for stuffing	15 pound
		Butter and oil	
1		onion, coarsely sliced	
1		garlic clove, crushed	
5	mL	each mace, rosemary and sage	1 teaspoon
4–6		slices side bacon	
		Boiling soup stock OR water	
		Heavy cream OR flour and water for thickening gravy	

1. Boil chestnuts in a saucepan until skins can be easily removed. Remove skins. Then reboil chestnuts until soft. Drain and mash.

2. Mix together beef, veal or pork, pork sausage, liver and gizzard and salt and pepper to taste. Add prunes, mashed chestnuts, and mix well.

3. Fry stuffing mixture very lightly in olive oil. Remove to a large mixing bowl, add grated cheese and raw eggs and combine well. Add 125 mL (½ cup) white wine.

4. Place stuffing into body and neck cavities of the turkey. Sew up all apertures carefully.

5. Preheat oven to 220°C (425°F).

6. Heat a few tablespoons each of oil and butter in a large roasting pan. Add the onion, garlic, mace, rosemary, sage and bacon slices. Place the turkey on top.

7. Roast turkey until brown (about 30 minutes). Lower heat to 180°C (350°F) and baste with remaining wine, which has been heated in a saucepan. Remove garlic clove.

8. Continue roasting until turkey is tender (about 3 hours), basting frequently with either boiling soup stock or water.

9. Remove turkey from pan. Pass the gravy through a fine wire sieve and thicken with a little cream or a paste made from flour and water. Heat over low heat until thickened, stirring constantly. Place turkey on a platter. Serve with hot gravy.

Makes 10 to 12 servings

Chicken and Peppers, Roman Style

POLLO E PEPE ALLA ROMANA

1		garlic clove, crushed	
1		onion, chopped	
30	mL	olive oil	2 tablespoons
2	kg	chicken pieces	4–4½ pounds
700	g	peeled ripe tomatoes OR 750 mL	1½ pounds
		canned tomatoes, drained	3 cups
700	g	green peppers, cut into	1½ pounds
		lengthwise strips	
		Salt and freshly ground pepper	

1. Sauté garlic and onions in oil until golden. Discard garlic.

2. Add chicken pieces and brown on all sides.

3. Add tomatoes, peppers, salt and pepper to taste. Cover and simmer until chicken is tender (40 minutes).

Makes 4 to 6 servings

Chicken, Finanziera Style

POLLO ALLA FINANZIERA

60	mL	chopped celery	4 tablespoons
45	mL	fresh chopped parsley	3 tablespoons
3		leaves fresh basil	
		OR pinch of dried basil	
1		onion, finely sliced	
1		carrot, diced	
125	mL	olive oil	½ cup
2.5	kg	chicken pieces	5 pounds
15	mL	all-purpose flour	1 tablespoon
125	mL	chicken broth	½ cup
125	mL	dry red wine	½ cup
		Salt and freshly ground pepper	
		Giblets OR chicken livers,	
		cut into small pieces (optional)	
250	g	sliced mushrooms	½ pound
125	mL	dry Marsala wine	½ cup

Trout with mushrooms garnished with lemon wedges, marjoram and mint. (Page 49).

1. In a large saucepan or Dutch oven, sauté celery, parsley, basil, onion and carrot in olive oil for 10 minutes; stir often to prevent burning.

2. Add chicken and cook over very low heat, uncovered, for 20 minutes, stirring occasionally. Remove chicken and keep warm.

3. Strain sauce and return liquid to the pot. Blend in flour, then slowly stir in chicken broth and red wine. Bring to a boil.

4. Return chicken to the pot, season with salt and pepper to taste, cover and simmer over low heat until chicken is tender.

5. Remove chicken to a warm serving dish.

6. Add giblets or livers, mushrooms and Marsala wine to sauce. Simmer uncovered until giblets or livers are cooked.

7. Pour sauce over chicken and serve.

Makes 4 to 5 servings

Rabbit with Green Olives
CONIGLIO CON OLIVE VERDI

30	mL	oil	2 tablespoons
125	g	pork belly, diced	4 ounces
		OR pancetta, diced	
2		onions, sliced	
1		medium-sized rabbit, cleaned and cut into serving pieces	
30	mL	all-purpose flour	2 tablespoons
500	mL	beef broth	2 cups
2		bay leaves	
		Pinch of rosemary	
		Salt and freshly ground pepper	
90	mL	green olives	⅓ cup
15	mL	capers	1 tablespoon

Chicken Finanziera served for centuries in the Finance Police barracks in the Italian Alps. (Page 54).

1. Heat oil in a saucepan and sauté pork and onions until onions are golden.

2. Add rabbit pieces and fry, turning often, until rabbit is lightly browned on all sides.

3. Sprinkle in flour and stir to blend. Gradually stir in beef broth. Add bay leaves, rosemary and salt and pepper to taste.

4. Bring to a boil, cover and reduce heat; simmer until tender (about 1 hour). Stir in olives and capers. Serve hot.

Makes 4 to 6 servings

Chicken Ghiottona

POLLO ALLA GHIOTTONA

2	kg	chicken pieces	4–4½ pounds
60	mL	butter	4 tablespoons
375	mL	dry white wine	1½ cups
250	mL	milk	1 cup
250	mL	tomato OR vegetable juice	1 cup
		Salt and freshly ground pepper	

1. Place all ingredients in a large pot. Bring to a boil, cover and cook over moderate heat until chicken is done (about 35 minutes). Serve with rice or polenta.

Makes 4 to 6 servings

MEAT

Pork Sausage with Grapes

SALSICCIA E UVA

This dish is especially popular during the grape season in Italy, when grapes are so plentiful.

12		sweet Italian sausages	
60	mL	butter	4 tablespoons
750	mL	white OR green grapes	3 cups

1. Puncture each sausage in about 3 places with a needle.

2. In a large frying pan, fry sausage in butter for 10 minutes, turning occasionally.

3. Add grapes and simmer 20 minutes with cover on.

Makes 6 servings

Steak with Caper Sauce
BISTECCA IN INTIGOLO DI CAPPERI

2.5	kg	porterhouse OR sirloin steak, thickly cut	5 pounds
10	mL	paprika	2 teaspoons
		Salt and freshly ground pepper	
3		onions, chopped	
125	mL	olive oil	½ cup
60	mL	capers	4 tablespoons
2		lemons	

1. Season steak slices with paprika, salt and pepper to taste.

2. In a large frying pan, sauté onions in oil for 5 minutes over low heat.

3. Raise heat, add steak and sear on both sides.

4. Reduce heat to medium and add capers; cook until meat is done to taste.

5. Sprinkle with the juice of 1 lemon and garnish with lemon wedges.

Makes 6 to 8 servings

Filet Mignon, Sicilian Style
FILETTO ALLA SICILIANA

In Sicily this dish is only served on the most special occasions because in the south there's very little beef.

2	kg	filet mignon	4 pounds
8		slices back bacon	
2		onions, sliced	
		Salt and freshly ground pepper	
125	mL	butter	½ cup
250	mL	Marsala wine	1 cup

1. Cut filet into slices 4-cm (1½-inches) thick.

2. In a heated frying pan, brown bacon slightly. In bacon drippings, sauté onions until golden brown. Remove bacon and onions.

3. Brown filet slices in bacon drippings over high heat (about 5 minutes on each side). Lower heat. Add salt and pepper to taste.

4. Melt butter in a separate pan. Pour over filet. Add Marsala and simmer 5 minutes uncovered. Serve with bacon and onions.

Makes 8 servings

Nonna Bettina's Beef Roll

INVOLTINI DI MANZO DI NONNA BETTINA (CON UOVA E PISELLI)

I was greatly honored when my dear friend Nonna Bettina shared with me her generations-old recipe for beef roll. At the time this book went to press, Nonna was still in charge of the family kitchen, at age 101.

2		slices top round, each weighing about 100 g and measuring about 15 × 25 cm	¼ pound 6 × 10 inches
4		slices ham	
4		leaves fresh sage OR 5 mL dried sage	1 teaspoon
4		hard-cooked eggs	
60	mL	butter	4 tablespoons
30	mL	olive oil	2 tablespoons
1		sprig fresh rosemary OR pinch of dried rosemary	
4–6		fresh carrots, sliced Salt Pinch of sugar	
15	mL	all-purpose flour	1 tablespoon
250	mL	beef broth OR water	1 cup
500	mL	frozen peas OR canned baby peas, drained	2 cups

1. Pound meat until thin.

2. On each beef slice, place 2 slices of ham (end to end), 2 leaves of fresh sage and 2 cooked eggs (if necessary trim points so they fit nicely tail to tail).

3. Roll the meat and ham around eggs and bind well with toothpicks or string.

4. Heat 30 mL (2 tablespoons) butter and olive oil in a frying pan and first add rosemary, then beef rolls. Brown meat all around and lower heat. Cover and simmer until meat is cooked (about 20 minutes). Stir occasionally to avoid sticking.

5. In a separate pot, sauté carrots in remaining butter. Add salt and sugar.

6. Make a paste out of flour and broth and add to carrots. Cook until carrots are tender but firm (about 15 to 20 minutes), stirring occasionally. Add peas to cooked carrots and cook until heated through.

7. Cut beef rolls into serving pieces, about 5 cm (2 inches) thick.

8. Place vegetables on a warm serving platter and arrange beef rolls, cut into serving pieces, on top. Pour pan gravy from beef rolls on top or serve separately over rice or potatoes.

Makes 3 to 4 servings

Breaded Pork Chops
COTOLETTE DI MAIALE IMPANATE

4		thick pork loin chops	
250	mL	wine vinegar	1 cup
		Salt and freshly ground pepper	
1		large egg	
15	mL	cold water	1 tablespoon
250	mL	bread crumbs	1 cup
1		garlic clove, chopped	
15	mL	fresh chopped parsley	1 tablespoon
60	mL	olive oil	4 tablespoons
125	mL	all-purpose flour	½ cup

1. In a shallow dish, marinate pork chops in vinegar for about 1 hour.

2. Remove chops and dry with absorbent toweling. Season with salt and pepper to taste.

3. Beat egg lightly and blend with cold water. Set aside.

4. Mix together bread crumbs, garlic, parsley and a little salt and pepper.

5. Heat oil in a large frying pan. Roll chops in flour, dip in egg, then in bread crumbs and fry over high heat until golden brown on both sides. Lower heat and cover. Cook until done (about 20 minutes). Turn frequently during cooking to avoid sticking.

Makes 4 servings

Lamb, Roman Style

AGNELLO ALLA ROMANA

3		garlic cloves	
3		anchovy fillets	
125	mL	wine vinegar	½ cup
1	kg	lean shoulder of lamb, cubed	2 pounds
		OR leg of lamb, cubed	
125	mL	all-purpose flour seasoned with	½ cup
		salt and freshly ground pepper	
60	mL	olive oil	4 tablespoons
1		sprig fresh rosemary	
		Salt and freshly ground pepper	

1. Mash garlic and anchovies with a pestle in a mortar until they form a paste. Place in a small mixing bowl and dilute with vinegar.

2. Dredge lamb with seasoned flour.

3. Heat oil and sprig of rosemary in a frying pan until it begins to smoke. Immediately remove rosemary and add lamb; brown on all sides. Remove lamb and keep warm. Season with salt and pepper to taste.

4. Add vinegar mixture to the frying pan and simmer uncovered until sauce is reduced by two-thirds.

5. Return lamb to frying pan and simmer about 10 minutes, stirring frequently. Serve hot.

Makes 4 to 6 servings

Italian Braised Beef

MANZO BRASATO

2–2.5	kg	chuck OR rump roast of beef	5 pounds
4		garlic cloves, thinly sliced	
		Salt and freshly ground pepper	
30	mL	olive oil	2 tablespoons
30	mL	butter	2 tablespoons
2		onions, thickly sliced	
2		carrots, sliced lengthwise	
1		stalk celery, cut into 2-cm pieces	1-inch
250	mL	fresh chopped parsley	1 cup
1 or 2		parings fresh lemon peel	

125	mL	tomato paste diluted with	½ cup
		250 mL water	1 cup
175	mL	red Burgundy wine	¾ cup

1. Cut slits into the meat and insert thin slices of garlic. Season meat with salt and pepper to taste.

2. In a large Dutch oven, heat oil and butter and brown the meat on all sides.

3. Add onions, carrots and celery and cook until browned.

4. Add parsley, lemon peel, tomato paste diluted with water and wine. Bring to a boil, cover and cook slowly until meat is tender (about 2 to 2½ hours). Stir occasionally to prevent meat from sticking.

5. Slice meat. Strain sauce and serve as gravy.

Makes 4 to 6 servings

Pork Supreme, Toscana Style

ARISTA DI MAIALE ALLA TOSCANA

1		loin of pork (2.5 kg)	(5 pounds)
10	mL	salt	2 teaspoons
5	mL	freshly ground pepper	1 teaspoon
15	mL	dried rosemary	1 tablespoon
4		garlic cloves, sliced	
750	mL	dry white wine	3 cups
		OR dry vermouth	
		Cornstarch OR flour (optional)	

1. Preheat oven to 230°C (450°F).

2. Trim excess fat off pork, but leave enough for pan juices. Rub with salt and pepper. Cut shallow slits in meat and insert rosemary and slices of garlic.

3. Tie roast securely with string and place fat side up in a roasting pan.

4. Brown in oven for about 45 minutes and pour off excess fat. Reduce heat to 180°C (350°F), pour wine over pork, and cover with aluminum foil. Cook until done (about 2 more hours), basting frequently.

5. Remove from oven and allow roast to stand in pan juices about 10 to 15 minutes. Remove string and serve. Slice meat. Serve with strained pan juices as gravy; or thicken juices with cornstarch or flour. Serve with red kidney beans cooked in red wine.

Makes 6 to 8 servings

Veal Scaloppine with Marsala

SCALOPPINE DI VITELLO AL MARSALA

500	g	veal scaloppine	1 pound
80	mL	all-purpose flour	⅓ cup
90	mL	butter	6 tablespoons
		Salt and freshly ground pepper	
50	mL	dry Marsala wine	¼ cup

1. Dredge the veal with flour.

2. Sauté in butter in a large frying pan for 2 to 3 minutes on each side. Add salt and pepper to taste and Marsala wine.

3. Simmer uncovered 2 more minutes and serve hot.

Makes 2 to 4 servings

Roast Leg of Lamb

AGNELLO ALLA SICILIANA

1		leg of lamb (3 kg)	(6 pounds)
3		leaves fresh mint, chopped	
		OR 30 mL dried mint	2 tablespoons
6		thick slices pancetta	
		OR back bacon	
15	mL	olive oil	1 tablespoon
2		onions, sliced	
3		carrots, sliced	
250	mL	hot water	1 cup

1. Preheat oven to 220°C (425°F). Cut meat away from bone about 5 cm (2 inches) and insert chopped mint and 1 slice pancetta.

2. Place lamb, fat-side up, in a shallow roasting pan brushed with oil and place the remaining pancetta on top. Arrange the onions and carrots around the meat.

3. Place lamb in oven and brown 15 minutes on each side basting occasionally. Add hot water and continue roasting until lamb is tender (30 minutes per pound), basting occasionally.

4. Carve lamb and serve hot with onions, carrots and a salad. Strain the pan liquid. Then strain most of the surface fat from drippings. Reheat and serve as gravy.

Makes 6 servings

VEGETABLES

Fried String Beans
FAGIOLIN VERDI FRITTI

500	g	fresh string beans	1 pound
125	mL	all-purpose flour	½ cup
		Olive oil for frying	
		Salt	

1. Parboil beans until tender but firm; do not overcook.

2. Roll in flour.

3. Heat oil in a frying pan and fry beans until crisp and golden brown. Season with salt and serve immediately.

Makes 4 servings

Spinach with Anchovies
SPINACI E ACCIUGHE

1	kg	fresh spinach	2 pounds
30	mL	butter	2 tablespoons
5		anchovies	
1		garlic clove, chopped	
		Freshly ground pepper	

1. Clean spinach and cook, covered, without water or salt until soft. Drain and finely chop.

2. Heat butter and sauté anchovies and garlic for a few minutes.

3. Return spinach to pan, add pepper to taste and cook until spinach is heated through, stirring frequently. Serve with triangles of fried bread.

Makes 4 servings

Brussels Sprouts with Egg Sauce
CAVOLINI DI BRUSSELLES CON SUGO D'UOVA

This is a wonderful accompaniment to pork. If Brussels sprouts are not in season, substitute green beans.

60	mL	butter	4 tablespoons
500	g	cooked Brussels sprouts	1 pound
250	mL	beef broth	1 cup
		Salt and freshly ground pepper	
2		eggs, beaten	
45	mL	dry white wine	3 tablespoons

1. Heat butter in a large frying pan and lightly sauté Brussels sprouts until they begin to change color. Set aside.

2. To make egg sauce, heat beef stock; add salt and pepper to taste, and beat in eggs with a wire whisk. Simmer very gently until mixture thickens, whisking constantly.

3. Remove sauce from heat. Whisk, add wine and whisk again.

4. Place Brussels sprouts on a serving platter. Pour egg sauce on top and serve.

Makes 4 servings

Pumpkin Sicilian
ZUCCA ALLA SICILIANA

45	mL	olive oil	3 tablespoons
1		garlic clove, crushed	
1	kg	pumpkin, peeled and sliced into julienne strips	2 pounds
500	mL	dry white wine	2 cups
		Salt	
500	mL	fresh mint leaves	2 cups
		OR 30 mL dried mint	2 tablespoons
125	mL	heavy cream	½ cup
		Juice of ½ lemon	
		Dash of pepper	

Nonna Bettina's beef rolls served on a sea of green peas. (Page 60).

1. Heat oil in a large saucepan and sauté garlic and pumpkin until pumpkin is slightly browned. Do not overcook.

2. Add wine, salt to taste and mint leaves and cook 2 minutes. Remove mint leaves.

3. Add cream and lemon juice and cook 5 minutes, uncovered, stirring constantly. Season with pepper and serve.

Makes 4 to 6 servings

Minted Zucchini
ZUCCHINI ALLA MENTA

4		medium-sized zucchini	
30	mL	olive oil	2 tablespoons
		Salt and freshly ground pepper	
15	mL	chopped fresh mint leaves,	1 tablespoon
		OR 5 mL dried mint	1 teaspoon

1. Parboil whole zucchinis in water for about 10 minutes and cut into long, thin strips.

2. Heat oil in a frying pan and add zucchini, salt and pepper to taste and mint. Cook 5 minutes, stirring frequently.

Makes 4 servings

Leeks Cacciocavallo
PORRI AL CACCIOCAVALLO

1	kg	fresh leeks	2 pounds
30	mL	oil for frying	2 tablespoons
2		slices side bacon, diced	
60	mL	all-purpose flour	4 tablespoons
250	mL	light cream OR milk	1 cup
		Salt and freshly ground pepper	
		Pinch of nutmeg	
1–2		eggs, beaten	
		Grated cacciocavallo cheese	

Stuffed eggplants in various stages of preparation. (Page 70).

1. Wash and trim leeks, leaving as much of the green as possible. Cook in salted boiling water until tender.

2. Preheat oven to 180°C (350°F).

3. Heat oil in a frying pan and fry bacon pieces. Sprinkle with flour, add cream or milk and cook over low to moderate heat, stirring constantly, until a smooth sauce has formed. Add salt and pepper to taste and nutmeg.

4. Remove from heat and beat in eggs with a wooden spoon.

5. Drain leeks and turn them into a greased casserole. Pour sauce on top, sprinkle generously with cheese and bake until cheese has browned (10 to 15 minutes).

Makes 4 servings

Stuffed Eggplants
MELANZANE RIPIENE

6	small pear-shaped eggplants	
3	tomatoes, peeled and chopped	
1	garlic clove, finely chopped	
2	anchovy fillets, chopped	
	Pinch of marjoram	
	Pinch of salt	
30	mL water	2 tablespoons
30	mL olive oil	2 tablespoons

1. Preheat oven to 180°C (350°F).

2. Remove stalk from each eggplant. From the same end spoon out 30 to 45 mL (2 to 3 tablespoons) of pulp and reserve.

3. Combine eggplant pulp, tomatoes, garlic, anchovies and marjoram and mix well. Stuff eggplants with the mixture.

4. Place stuffed eggplants on their side in a medium-sized baking pan; add salt, water and oil to the pan and bake uncovered 40 to 50 minutes. If pan dries out, add more water. Serve hot.

Makes 6 servings

Variation: You can also stuff eggplants with a mixture of 3 tomatoes, peeled and chopped, and 125 mL ($\frac{1}{2}$ cup) each diced salami and grated Romano cheese.

Broccoli with Black Olives
BROCCOLI E OLIVE NERE

2		bunches fresh broccoli	
75	mL	olive oil	5 tablespoons
2		garlic cloves, crushed	
250	mL	pitted black olives, chopped	1 cup
		Grated Romano OR Parmesan cheese (optional)	

1. Cut and trim the broccoli into flowerets with short stems. Cook in boiling salted water or steam until tender, but firm. Don't overcook. Drain.

2. Heat oil in a frying pan and sauté garlic until golden brown. Discard garlic. Add olives and stir-fry about 1 minute.

3. Add broccoli. Stir, cover and cook over low heat until heated through.

4. Serve hot. If desired, sprinkle with grated cheese.

Makes 6 servings

Cabbage cooked in Wine
CAVOLI COTTI NEL VINO

1		large cabbage, quartered	
45	mL	olive oil	3 tablespoons
1		grated onion	
250	mL	boiling water	1 cup
		Salt	
		Pinch of sugar	
250	mL	white wine	1 cup
15	mL	capers	1 tablespoon

1. Soak cabbage in cold salted water for 30 minutes. Drain and coarsely shread.

2. Heat oil in a large saucepan and brown the onion. Add cabbage and stir well.

3. Stir in boiling water, salt to taste, sugar, wine and capers.

4. Cover and cook over low heat until cabbage is tender (about 15 to 20 minutes). If necessary, drain cabbage before serving.

Makes 4 to 6 servings

Peppers with Tomatoes and Onions

PEPERONI CON POMIDORO E CIPOLLE

This is delicious served hot on rice or cold the next day between two slices of bread.

8		large peppers (red OR green OR yellow OR mixed)	
60	mL	oil	4 tablespoons
3		onions, chopped	
3		garlic cloves, chopped	
2		bay leaves	
4		large tomatoes, peeled and quartered	
		Salt and freshly ground pepper	

1. Cut peppers lengthwise into very thin julienne strips and rinse in cold water.

2. Heat oil and sauté onions, garlic and bay leaves slowly for 5 minutes, stirring frequently. Add peppers and mix well. Cover and cook slowly, about 15 minutes.

3. Add tomatoes and salt and pepper to taste. Cook uncovered, stirring frequently, until most liquid has evaporated and sauce has thickened (about 30 minutes).

4. Remove bay leaves and serve either hot or cold.

Makes 6 to 8 servings

Creamed Onions

CIPOLLE ALLA CREMA

This is a tasty side dish with mutton.

1	kg	small white onions, peeled	2 pounds
		Salt and freshly ground pepper	
15	mL	all-purpose flour	1 tablespoon
30	mL	cold water	2 tablespoons
125	mL	dry white wine	$\frac{1}{2}$ cup
		Good pinch of nutmeg	

1. Place whole onions in a large saucepan. Cover with water and add salt and pepper to taste.

2. Bring to a boil, reduce heat to moderate, and cook uncovered until onions are tender but firm (about 20 to 25 minutes).

3. Make a paste by combining flour with water and add to onion stock. Heat and stir with a wooden spoon until liquid thickens.

4. Add wine and nutmeg. Cook 15 minutes, stirring often.

Makes 6 servings

Asparagus Parmesan
ASPARAGI ALLA PARMIGIANA

1.5	kg	fresh young asparagus	3 pounds
1	L	lightly salted boiling water	1 quart
175	mL	melted sweet butter	¾ cup
175	mL	grated Parmesan cheese	¾ cup

1. Preheat oven to 230°C (450°F).

2. Wash asparagus and trim the bottoms. Place in a large casserole with about 2.5 cm (1 inch) boiling water; do not completely cover with water.

3. Bake loosely covered with aluminum foil until stalks are tender but still firm (10 minutes). Remove from oven and drain well.

4. Place one layer of asparagus in a buttered glass baking dish; brush with melted butter and sprinkle lightly with Parmesan cheese. Repeat until ingredients are used up, finishing with a layer of Parmesan cheese.

5. Bake uncovered for about 5 minutes and serve immediately.

Makes 6 servings

Sweet and Sour Zucchini
ZUCCHINE AGRO DOLCE

6		medium-sized zucchini	
125	mL	peanut oil	½ cup
		Salt and freshly ground pepper	
45	mL	wine vinegar	3 tablespoons
15	mL	sugar	1 tablespoon
15	mL	fresh chopped sweet basil	1 tablespoon
		OR 5 mL dried sweet basil	1 teaspoon

1. Wash zucchini and scrape lightly. Cut crosswise into 1-cm ($\frac{1}{2}$-inch) slices.

2. Heat oil and fry zucchini until tender and slightly brown (about 3 minutes on each side).

3. Remove zucchini to a deep bowl. Add salt and pepper to taste.

4. Add vinegar and sugar to oil in frying pan. Cook over low heat for 2 minutes and pour over zucchini. Sprinkle with chopped basil. Serve hot or cold.

Makes 4 to 6 servings

Cauliflower with Lemon Sauce
CAVOLFIORI AL SUCCO DI LIMONE

1		**large cauliflower**	
30	mL	**butter**	2 tablespoons
30	mL	**all-purpose flour**	2 tablespoons
2		**egg yolks, beaten**	
		Juice of $\frac{1}{2}$ lemon	
		Salt and freshly ground pepper	

1. Soak cauliflower, head down, in cold salted water for 30 minutes.

2. Separate into flowerets and cook in boiling salted water until tender. Drain, reserving the liquid, and keep hot.

3. Make a roux by melting butter over low heat in a small saucepan; add flour and stir well with a wooden spoon. Add 1 cup of the cauliflower water and mix well.

4. In a small bowl, beat egg yolks and lemon juice with a wire whisk until frothy.

5. Remove sauce from the heat and whisk in the egg and lemon mixture. Add seasonings and reheat, whisking constantly, until thickened.

6. Pour sauce over cauliflower and serve.

Makes 6 servings

THIRD COURSE – SALADS

The third course is salad, usually marked by its simplicity. Fresh, crisp greens such as endive, lettuce, spinach, chicory or chard are common bases embellished with tomatoes, cucumbers, zucchini, mushrooms, celery or Italian cheeses. Fragrant fresh herbs such as parsley, basil, mint and garlic are the final, irresistible touch. The most common dressings are a simple blend of olive oil, wine vinegar, salt and freshly ground pepper.

The salads included in this section are the exception, rather than the rule. Many are substantial enough to serve as a luncheon or supper main dish.

Green Bean Salad
INSALATA DI FAGIOLINI VERDI

500	g	fresh green beans	1 pound
60	mL	olive oil	4 tablespoons
30	mL	vinegar	2 tablespoons
1		garlic clove, finely chopped	
		Salt and freshly ground pepper	

1. Clean beans and trim off ends. Cook to desired tenderness. Drain and cut in half.

2. Place beans in a salad bowl. Add oil, vinegar, garlic, salt and pepper to taste.

3. Toss. Serve warm or chilled.

Makes 4 servings

Variation: You can also use wax beans or a mixture of wax and green beans.

Tomato with Mozzarella and Basil
INSALATA DI POMODORO, MOZZARELLA E BASILICO

In Italy this salad is often served with the prosciutto and melon course, but it also makes a delightful first course for lunch or dinner. If fresh basil isn't available, substitute dry basil soaked in equal parts of olive oil and lemon juice for one hour.

6		ripe tomatos	
		Salt	
700	g	fresh mozzarella cheese, cut into	1½ pounds
		2.5-cm cubes	1-inch
125	mL	olive oil	½ cup
		Freshly ground pepper	
250	mL	coarsely chopped fresh basil	1 cup
		OR 30 mL dried basil	2 tablespoons

1. Cut tomatoes in half. Squeeze gently to remove seeds and juice. Salt and let stand face down on absorbent toweling about 20 minutes. Cut into wedges.

2. Place tomato wedges, cheese cubes, oil, salt and pepper to taste into a salad bowl and toss.

3. Add basil and toss gently before serving.

Makes 6 to 8 servings

Pear, Cheese and Walnut Salad
INSALATA DI FORMAGGIO, PERE E NOCI

12		pears, peeled, cored and	
		thinly sliced	
500	g	gorgonzola cheese, crumbled	1 pound
		OR gruyère, cubed	
125	mL	walnut pieces	½ cup
250	mL	fresh lemon juice	1 cup

1. Mix pears, cheese and walnuts together.
2. Add lemon juice and toss.

Makes 12 servings

Tomato with mozzarella and basil on lettuce leaves. (Above).

Squid Salad

INSALATA DI CALAMARI

Traditionally this dish is served on Christmas Eve with a glass of new wine and fresh Italian bread.

1	kg	fresh OR frozen squid	2 pounds
2	L	boiling water	2 quarts
60	mL	olive oil	4 tablespoons
		Juice of 1 large lemon	
15	mL	chopped fresh mint	1 tablespoon
1		garlic clove, finely chopped	
		Salt and freshly ground pepper	
		Lettuce leaves	

1. Clean squid if fresh (frozen may already be cleaned), and cut into bite-sized pieces. Cook in boiling water until tender (about 30 minutes). Drain. Place in a large mixing bowl.

2. In a separate bowl, combine oil, lemon juice, mint, garlic and salt and pepper to taste. Pour over squid and chill at least 4 hours, preferably overnight, before serving.

3. Serve cold on lettuce leaves.

Makes 4 to 6 servings

Italian Potato Salad

INSALATA DI PATATE ALL'ITALIANA

8		medium-sized potatoes, cooked in their skins	
2		hard-cooked eggs, chopped	
4		anchovy fillets, chopped	
1		large onion, chopped	
1		green pepper, chopped	
		Salt and freshly ground pepper	
125	mL	Italian dressing (See below)	½ cup
1		garlic clove	
6–8		lettuce leaves	

Pear, cheese and walnut salad. In this variation, canned pear halves are filled with a creamed mixture of gorgonzola and ricotta, topped with walnuts. (Page 76).

1. Peel potatoes and cut into cubes or slices.

2. In a large mixing bowl, combine potatoes, eggs, anchovies, onion and green pepper. Add salt and pepper to taste and enough Italian dressing to bind salad together.

3. Rub a wooden bowl with garlic. Arrange lettuce at bottom and add 15 mL (1 tablespoon) Italian dressing. Toss until leaves are coated.

4. Place potato salad on top of lettuce. Chill before serving.

Makes 6 servings

Italian Dressing
CONDIMENTO PER INSALATA

75	mL	olive oil	6 tablespoons
50	mL	wine vinegar	¼ cup
		Salt and freshly ground pepper	

1. Combine oil, vinegar and salt and pepper to taste. Mix in a blender or shake well in a glass jar with a tight-fitting lid.

Makes 125 mL (½ cup)

Rice Salad with Asparagus and Mushrooms
INSALATA DI RISO, ASPARAGI E FUNGHI

This dish originated in northern Italy, where it is usually served with chicken.

1	L	chicken broth	1 quart
500	mL	uncooked long-grain Italian rice	2 cups
500	g	fresh asparagus, cooked until tender and cut into bite-sized pieces	1 pound
500	mL	diced celery	2 cups
500	mL	thinly sliced fresh mushrooms	2 cups
4		hard-cooked eggs	
		Pinch of salt	
		Pinch of freshly ground white pepper	
5	mL	paprika	1 teaspoon
3	mL	Dijon mustard	½ teaspoon
250	mL	olive oil	1 cup
30	mL	heavy cream	2 tablespoons

45	mL	fresh lemon juice	3 tablespoons
5	mL	dry Marsala wine	1 teaspoon
		OR dry white vermouth	

1. In a large saucepan, bring chicken broth to a boil. Add rice and cook covered until rice is tender but firm. Drain rice, reserving liquid, and place in a salad bowl. Let cool.

2. To broth add asparagus, celery, mushrooms and mashed yolks of hard-cooked eggs. Season with salt, white pepper, paprika, mustard and mix.

3. Add the oil, drop by drop, stirring constantly (as though you were making mayonnaise), until oil is used up.

4. Add cream, lemon juice, Marsala or vermouth and chopped egg white and mix again. Add to cold rice and toss.

Makes 4 to 6 servings

Macaroni Salad

INSALATA DI MACCHERONI

4		firm ripe tomatoes, sliced	
3		anchovy fillets	
125	mL	pitted black olives, coarsely chopped	½ cup
125	mL	pitted green olives, coarsely chopped	½ cup
150	g	fresh ricotta cheese	5 ounces
125	mL	olive oil	½ cup
		Salt and freshly ground pepper	
5	mL	oregano	1 teaspoon
675	g	short pasta, such as pennetta	1½ pounds

1. Combine tomatoes, anchovies, olives and ricotta cheese in a large salad bowl. Add oil and toss. Season with salt and pepper to taste and oregano and toss again. Set aside for 1 hour.

2. After 1 hour, cook pasta in a large pot of salted boiling water until desired tenderness. Drain well; then wash with cold water and drain again.

3. Add pasta to tomato mixture. Toss and serve or chill first.

Makes 6 servings

Vegetable Salad

INSALATA VERDE

This layered salad is as delightful to look at as it is delectable to eat.

SALAD

1		small cauliflower, separated into flowerets	
4		carrots, sliced	
250	g	potatoes, peeled and sliced	½ pound
3–4		radishes, sliced	
125	g	mushrooms, sliced	¼ pound
250	g	green beans, cut in half	½ pound
6		stalks celery, chopped	
250	g	fresh peas	½ pound
		OR 1 can (300 g) peas, drained	(10 ounces)
		Boiling salted water	
1		large arrowroot cookie (15–20 cm) (optional)	(6–8 inches)
1		garlic clove	

DRESSING

1		garlic clove	
30	mL	fresh chopped parsley	2 tablespoons
60	mL	capers	4 tablespoons
2		hard-cooked egg yolks	
30	mL	soft bread crumbs	2 tablespoons
250	mL	grated fennel (optional)	½ cup
30	mL	lemon juice	2 tablespoons
		Olive oil	
		Salt and freshly ground pepper	

1. Cook all vegetables in boiling salted water until tender, but firm.

2. Rub the large arrowroot cookie with garlic and use it as the base for the salad, arranging all the vegetables on top in a colorful pyramid; or, attractively layer salad in a glass bowl.

3. To make dressing, combine garlic, parsley, capers, egg yolks, bread crumbs and fennel in blender and blend to a smooth paste. Gradually add lemon juice, enough oil to reach the desired consistency and salt and pepper to taste. Pour over salad and serve.

Makes 6 to 8 servings

Note: Pieces of smoked salmon, lobster, shrimps, smoked oysters, mackerel, sardines or anchovies can be added to the salad or used as garnishes. Create your own masterpiece.

Red and Green Tomato Salad

INSALATA DI POMODORI ROSSO E VERDI

4		medium-sized ripe tomatoes, cut in half	
1		medium-sized green tomato, cut in half	
8	mL	salt	1½ teaspoons
60	mL	olive oil	4 tablespoons
30	mL	fresh lemon juice	2 tablespoons
1–2	mL	garlic, finely chopped	¼ teaspoon
		Pinch of freshly ground pepper	

1. Squeeze tomato halves gently to remove seeds and juice. Sprinkle with salt and place face down on absorbent toweling. Let stand 20 minutes.

2. Slice tomatoes thickly and place in a salad bowl.

3. Mix together the oil, lemon juice, garlic and pepper and pour over tomatoes. Toss and let stand at least 20 minutes before serving.

Makes 6 servings

Orange and Lemon Salad

INSALATA DI ARANCE E LIMONI

This dish originated in Sicily, where the rinds of oranges and lemons are often eaten along with the fruit. The salad is especially nice after fish.

2		large lemons	
3		large oranges	
30	mL	olive oil	2 tablespoons
4		leaves fresh mint, chopped	
		OR 5 mL dried mint, soaked in wine for 1 hour	1 teaspoon
		Salt and freshly ground pepper	
10–12		lettuce leaves	

1. Wash unpeeled fruit and cut into slices as preferred.

2. Pour olive oil over fruit and toss. Sprinkle with mint, salt and pepper to taste, and toss again. Let stand for 20 minutes.

3. Arrange lettuce leaves on a platter and place fruit on top.

Makes 4 to 6 servings

DESSERTS

Dessert is considered an aftercourse dish, seldom served on a regular basis. When served, dessert generally comprises fresh fruit in season and cheese.

Cakes and pastries are not served with meals. Instead, they are saved for late afternoon breaks with coffee or wine.

Whether or not dessert follows the meal, espresso coffee provides the finale. Coffee became popular in Italy in the sixteenth century and has been a favorite beverage ever since; particularly espresso, a fine, dark grind brewed in special espresso makers. Espresso coffee is very strong and bitter, requiring lots of sugar or a sweet liqueur such as strega or cognac. Poured into special espresso glasses or demi-tasse cups, it may be topped with whipped cream or served with a strip of lemon peel on the side.

In the morning, espresso is mixed with hot milk as cappuccino and served with sugar and perhaps a dash of nutmeg or cinnamon.

Genoa Honey Jelly
GELATINA DI MIELE ALLA GENOVESE

560	mL	milk	2¼ cups
45	mL	honey	3 tablespoons
15	mL	unflavored gelatin	1 tablespoon
30	mL	cold water	2 tablespoons
15	mL	very strong espresso, cold	1 tablespoon
		OR thick Turkish coffee, cold	
		Almonds OR walnuts	
		Jelly fruits	

1. Heat milk with honey and stir until blended. Cool.

2. Add gelatin to cold water; add coffee. Heat just until gelatin dissolves.

3. Stir gelatin mixture into the milk.

4. Pour into a wet 25-cm (10-inch) tube pan and refrigerate until jelly is firm.

5. Set pan in hot water for a few seconds, unmould and decorate with nuts and jelly fruits. Slice into wedges and serve.

Makes 1 25-cm (10-inch) mould

Sponge Cake
PAN DI SPAGNA

This cake is a treat right out of the oven or it can be used as the base for other desserts, such as cassata or fruit flan.

300	mL	granulated sugar	1¼ cups
330	mL	all-purpose flour	1⅓ cups
8		egg yolks	
30	mL	water	2 tablespoons
10	mL	grated lemon rind	2 teaspoons
8	mL	almond extract	1½ teaspoons
8		egg whites	
		Pinch of salt	
		Icing sugar	

1. Preheat over to 180°C (350°F). Sift half the sugar with all the flour several times until well mixed. Set aside.

2. In a separate bowl, lightly beat together the egg yolks, water, lemon rind and almond extract.

3. Gradually sift the flour and sugar mixture over the egg mixture and fold in gently.

4. In another bowl, beat the egg whites until foamy. Add salt and remaining granulated sugar and beat until stiff.

5. Pour into an ungreased 25-cm (10-inch) tube pan and bake until cake is done (45 minutes). Do not jar during baking, or cake will fall.

6. Invert cake, while still in pan, onto a wire rack for 10 to 15 minutes. Remove from pan, dust with icing sugar and serve.

Makes one 10-inch cake.

Fruit Flan

SFORMATO DI FRUTTA

PASTRY

250	mL	all-purpose flour	1 cup
75	mL	fruit sugar	⅓ cup
125	mL	butter, at room temperature	½ cup
2–3	mL	finely grated lemon rind	½ teaspoon
2		large egg yolks, beaten	

1. Sift flour and sugar into a mound on a pastry board.

2. Make a hole in the centre and place in it the butter, lemon rind and egg yolks.

3. With the tips of your fingers, gradually draw the flour into the middle until the ingredients are well mixed. Knead into a firm dough (about 20 minutes). No water should be necessary. (You can also knead in your food processor. Follow manufacturer's instructions).

4. Wrap in waxed paper and chill for an hour before rolling.

PASTRY CREAM

300	mL	milk	½ pint
50	mL	fruit sugar	¼ cup
30	mL	all-purpose flour	2 tablespoons
2		egg yolks	
		Pinch of finely grated lemon rind	
15	mL	butter	1 tablespoon

1. Pour three-quarters of the milk into a saucepan and heat *almost* to boiling; do not boil.

2. In a bowl, combine sugar, flour, egg yolks, lemon rind and the remaining milk; mix thoroughly with a whisk. Add the hot milk, whisking constantly.

3. Place mixture in a saucepan and bring it *almost* to boiling, whisking constantly. Add the butter and blend.

4. Pour mixture into a bowl and cool, stirring occasionally to prevent a skin from forming.

Note: If necessary this cream can be thinned by adding more milk or it can be flavored with liqueur or spirits.

FRUIT FILLING

15–30	mL	strega	1–2 tablespoons
1		can (400 mL) dark Bing cherries OR any other fruit	(14 ounces)
15	mL	arrowroot OR gelatin	1 tablespoon
1		slice pineapple, cut into pieces (optional)	
12		candied cherries	
500	g	pitted dates	1 pound

1. Preheat oven to 190°C (375°F).

2. Roll pastry out thin and line a 23-cm (9-inch) flan pan or pie plate.

3. Prick it lightly, cover with waxed paper and weight it with dried peas or beans.

4. Bake in centre of oven for 20 minutes, removing the waxed paper and peas or beans after the first 10 minutes. Allow to cool.

5. Combine pastry cream with strega and spread over pastry.

6. Drain the canned fruit and retain 200 mL (¾ cup) of the juice. Blend arrowroot with one-third of the fruit juice. Bring remaining juice to a boil and stir in the arrowroot mixture. Bring mixture back to a boil, stirring constantly, and remove from heat when sauce is thick and smooth.

7. Decoratively arrange the fruit on the pastry cream.

8. When thickened juice has cooled slightly, spoon it over the fruit to form a glaze and chill to set.

Makes 8 to 10 servings

Note: Whipped ricotta may be used for decorating. Use a decorating tube.

Marsala Ice Cream
GELATO DI CREMA AL MARSALA

3		egg yolks	
90	mL	granulated sugar	6 tablespoons
90	mL	Marsala wine	6 tablespoons
1		large egg white, room temperature	
200	mL	whipping cream	⅓ pint

1. In a mixing bowl combine egg yolks and sugar. Beat thoroughly with a wire whisk. Add Marsala wine gradually and continue beating.

2. Place mixture in the top part of a double boiler over boiling water and heat 5 to 8 minutes, beating vigorously until mixture is thick and foamy.

3. Remove from heat immediately and let cool, whisking occasionally.

4. In a small bowl, beat egg white until stiff. In a chilled bowl, whip the cream until stiff. Gently fold the whipped cream, then the egg white into the cooled Marsala mixture. When thoroughly combined, place in a plastic freezer container, cover and freeze until firm, about 4 hours.

Makes 4 servings

Frozen Rum Sponge Cake Soufflé
TORTA SOUFFLE AL RUM

600	mL	chocolate ice cream	1 pint
250	g	black Bing cherries, pitted	½ pound
		OR 1 can (400 mL), drained	(14 ounces)
1		sponge cake (see recipe, page 85), cut into 1-cm slices	½-inch
175	mL	light amber rum	¾ cup
600	mL	vanilla ice cream	1 pint
1		large banana, peeled and thinly sliced	

1. Line the bottom of a chilled 2.25-litre (10-cup) soufflé dish with chocolate ice cream.

2. Cover with cherries and then a layer of sponge cake slices. Pour about a third of the rum over the cake layer.

3. Continue layering with vanilla ice cream, then banana slices followed by another layer of cake slices. Soak with remaining rum.

4. Cover with waxed paper and freeze at least six hours.

5. Remove from freezer and dip mould in hot water for 3 to 4 seconds. Remove waxed paper, unmould and slice.

Makes 6 to 8 servings

Fruit flan: black cherries, traditionally used in this recipe, are shown with a border of dates and decorative circles of whipped ricotta. (Page 86).

Cheese Cake
TORTA DI RICOTTA

PASTRY

500	mL	all-purpose flour	2 cups
2	mL	salt	½ teaspoon
150	mL	butter	⅔ cup
30	mL	dry sherry	2 tablespoons
		OR dry Marsala wine	

1. Sift together flour and salt.

2. Cut in butter with pastry blender until the consistency of coarse cornmeal. Stir in a little sherry at a time until dough holds. Add water if necessary to make a dough that sticks together. Pack dough into a ball. (Or, make dough in food processor; follow manufacturer's directions.)

3. Butter a 25-cm (10-inch) springform pan. Then roll out pastry in a circle to fit pan bottom and sides. Place pastry into pan.

FILLING

125	g	slivered toasted almonds	¼ pound
1	kg	ricotta cheese	2 pounds
4		eggs	
75	mL	sugar	⅓ cup
5	mL	vanilla	1 teaspoon
60	mL	liquid honey	¼ cup
		Pine nuts OR slivered almonds (optional)	

1. Preheat over to 180°C (350°F).

2. Combine almond slivers and ricotta cheese; mix thoroughly until smooth in a blender or with an electric mixer.

3. In a separate bowl, beat the eggs and sugar and blend in the vanilla. Add cheese mixture and blend well.

4. Pour into the crust. (Filling should be about 5 cm (2 inches) deep).

5. Drizzle half the honey over the top. If desired, sprinkle with pine nuts or slivered almonds.

6. Bake until filling is set and crust is golden (25 to 30 minutes). Drizzle remaining honey over cake and allow to cool.

Makes 10 to 12 servings

Cheese cake topped with fresh ripe figs for added effect. (Above).

Siena Fruit Cake

TORTA DI FRUTTA ALLA SIENESE

You'll need a good strong knife to cut through this "cake." It's only about 2.5 cm (1 inch) high and has the consistency of nougat. Traditionally it's served at Christmas.

150	mL	sifted all-purpose flour	⅔ cup
375	mL	almonds, coarsely chopped and lightly toasted	1½ cups
150	mL	hazelnuts, coarsely chopped and lightly toasted	⅔ cup
75	g	candied citron peel	3 ounces
75	g	candied orange peel	3 ounces
100	g	candied pumpkin OR melon peel	4 ounces
50	mL	cocoa	¼ cup
10	mL	freshly ground pepper	2 teaspoons
13	mL	cinnamon	2½ teaspoons
3	mL	vanilla extract	½ teaspoon
125	mL	honey	½ cup
75	mL	sugar	⅓ cup
30	mL	icing sugar	2 tablespoons

1. Preheat over to 150°C (300°F).

2. In a large mixing bowl, combine flour, almonds, hazelnuts, candied peels, cocoa, pepper, 8 mL (1½ teaspoons) of cinnamon and vanilla.

3. Heat honey and sugar in a large saucepan over low heat and stir constantly with a wooden spoon until a drop of the mixture forms a soft ball in cold water.

4. Remove syrup from stove and stir in the nut-flour mixture. Blend well.

5. Line the bottom and sides of a round 25-cm (10-inch) cake pan with greased waxed paper and spoon in batter. Bake 35 minutes. Remove from oven and let cool to room temperature.

6. Remove cake from pan and remove waxed paper. Sprinkle with a mixture of icing sugar and 5 mL (1 teaspoon) cinnamon. Cut with a strong knife and serve, or store covered in a cool place. Stays fresh for months.

Makes 1 25-cm (10-inch) cake

Honey Paste with Puff Pastry
PASTA DI MIELE IN PASTICCIO SOUFFLE

150	mL	all-purpose flour	$\frac{2}{3}$ cup
5	mL	baking powder	1 teaspoon
150	mL	ricotta cheese	$\frac{2}{3}$ cup
150	mL	butter OR margarine, softened	$\frac{2}{3}$ cup
5	mL	salt	1 teaspoon
		Honey	
125	mL	blanched slivered almonds	$\frac{1}{2}$ cup
50	mL	candied cherries	$\frac{1}{4}$ cup

1. To make puff pastry: Sift together flour and baking powder into a mixing bowl. Add ricotta cheese, butter and salt and knead until smooth and elastic (about 15 minutes).

2. On a well-floured cloth, roll out dough, then work back into a ball, roll out again and work into a ball again. Wrap in waxed paper and refrigerate about 20 minutes.

3. Preheat oven to 190°C (375°F).

4. Roll out puff pastry very thin, about the size of a large pizza.

5. Coat pastry with desired amount of honey and top with blanched almonds and candied cherries. Roll up tightly and cut into finger-thick slices. Place on their side on a greased baking sheet and bake 15 minutes or until crisp and golden.

Makes 12 to 24 servings

Coffee Ice Cream
GELATO DI CREMA DI CAFFE

250	mL	strong espresso coffee	1 cup
500	mL	heavy cream	2 cups
4		eggs, beaten	
375	mL	sugar	$1\frac{1}{2}$ cups
		Whipped cream for topping	

1. Combine coffee and heavy cream. Heat until almost boiling. (Do not boil.)

2. Cool slightly and slowly add eggs and sugar, whisking constantly. Cook uncovered in top of double boiler over boiling water, stirring constantly, until mixture becomes thick and smooth.

3. Cool and freeze at least 4 hours. Serve in sherbet glasses topped with whipped cream.

Makes 4 servings

Marsala Custard
CREMA ZABAIONE AL MARSALA

Marsala custard, or zabaione, is one of the best-known Italian sweet puddings. It's delicious served hot or as a cold custard over fruit.

12		egg yolks	
150	mL	sugar	⅔ cup
		Pinch of cinnamon	
		Scraped vanilla bean (5 cm long)	(2 inches long)
		OR 10 ml vanilla extract	2 teaspoons
375	mL	dry Marsala wine	1½ cups

1. Beat together egg yolks, sugar, cinnamon and vanilla with a whisk or electric beater until smooth.

2. Place in top part of double boiler over boiling water and, constantly whisking, heat until mixture is frothy and pale yellow (2 to 3 minutes).

3. Gradually add Marsala wine, beating constantly, and continue heating until hot, but do not boil. Remove vanilla bean and serve hot; or allow to cool, refrigerate and serve cold.

Makes 4 to 6 servings

Lugano Apple Tart
TORTA DI MELE ALLA LUGANO

PASTRY

250	mL	all purpose flour	1 cup
		Pinch of salt	
185	mL	butter	¾ cup
2		egg yolks	
30	mL	cream	2 tablespoons

FILLING

6		medium-sized apples, peeled, cored and sliced	
75	mL	butter, softened	⅓ cup
45	mL	sugar	3 tablespoons
5	mL	grated orange rind	1 teaspoon
5	mL	cinnamon	1 teaspoon
185	mL	white wine	¾ cup
		Honey	

1. Preheat oven to 220°C (425°F).

2. Make a pie pastry with flour, salt, butter, egg yolks and cream. (See Fruit Flan for method, page 86).

3. Roll out dough and place in a 1-L (9-inch) deep-dish pie plate. Trim excess around edges and save for lattice top.

4. Partially bake crust for 5 minutes. Reduce heat to 190°C (375°F). Allow to cool before filling.

5. In a saucepan, combine apples, butter, sugar, orange rind, cinnamon and white wine. Bring to a boil, cover, and steam until wine evaporates and fruit is tender, but firm.

6. Place filling in pastry shell and generously coat with honey.

7. Cut remaining pastry into strips. Arrange over pie filling in a lattice design. Seal edges.

8. Bake until pastry is light brown (about 30 minutes).

Makes 8 servings

Honey Almond Salami
INVOLTINI DI MANDORE MIELE

This is a rich, sumptuous after-dinner sweet to serve with espresso coffee.

500	g	almonds, coarsely chopped	1 pound
250	mL	granulated sugar	1 cup
125	mL	honey	½ cup
30–45	mL	grated chocolate	2–3 tablespoons
		Pinch of grated nutmeg	
		Pinch of cinnamon	
		Few drops of rosewater	
		Granulated sugar	

1. In a large mixing bowl, combine almonds, sugar, honey and grated chocolate.

2. Season with nutmeg, cinnamon and rosewater.

3. On a board lightly covered with granulated sugar, roll into a thick "sausage."

4. Wrap in waxed paper and refrigerate for 4 days.

5. Slice and, if desired, place in paper casings before serving.

Makes 12 to 24 servings

Biscuit Tortoni
BISCOTTI TORTONI

This easy-to-make dessert tastes as good as it looks.

375	mL	crushed toasted almonds	1½ cups
125	mL	crushed macaroons	½ cup
500	mL	whipping cream	2 cups
45	mL	dark rum	3 tablespoons
50	mL	icing sugar	¼ cup
3–4		maraschino cherries, halved	

1. Combine all but 30 mL (2 tablespoons) of the crushed almonds, all the macaroons and half the cream. Mix well.

2. In a separate bowl, whip remaining cream with rum and sugar until stiff.

3. Fold almond-macaroon mixture into whipped cream.

4. Spoon into 6 or 8 paper dessert cups and freeze until firm, about 4 hours.

5. Top each with half a cherry, a sprinkle of toasted almonds and return to freezer until ready to serve.

Makes 6 to 8 servings

Lemon Ice, Roman Style
GELATO DI LIMONE ALLA ROMANA

This ice, made with fresh lemon juice, is particularly refreshing.

550	mL	sugar	2¼ cups
1	L	water	1 quart

250	mL	fresh lemon juice, strained through a sieve	1 cup
1		egg white	
30	mL	rum	2 tablespoons

1. Heat 500 mL (2 cups) of sugar and all the water over moderate heat until sugar dissolves. Stir in lemon juice.

2. Pour mixture into a freezer container and freeze until mushy, stirring frequently.

3. Beat egg white and remaining sugar until stiff, slowly adding rum while beating.

4. Fold mixture into partially frozen lemon ice and continue freezing; stir often until frozen to a sherbet consistency.

5. Spoon into sherbet glasses and serve.

Makes 4 servings

Sicilian Cassata
TORTA DI CREMA ALLA SICILIANA

CAKE

| 1 | | sponge cake (25 cm) (see recipe, page 85) | (10 inches) |

FILLING

750	g	ricotta cheese	1½ pounds
125	mL	granulated sugar	½ cup
30	g	grated unsweetened chocolate	1 ounce
10	mL	almond extract	2 teaspoons

ICING

250–375	mL	icing sugar	1–1½ cups
1		egg white	
5	mL	almond extract	1 teaspoon
5	mL	fresh lemon juice	1 teaspoon

DECORATION

30	g	grated unsweetened chocolate	1 ounce
50	mL	candied mixed fruits, finely chopped	¼ cup
50	mL	finely chopped walnuts	¼ cup

1. Slice the sponge cake into 3 layers of equal thickness.

2. To make filling: mix ricotta cheese and granulated sugar in blender or food processor until smooth and creamy. Stir in grated chocolate and almond extract and refrigerate until ready to use.

3. Place bottom layer of cake on a round plate and spread with half the filling mixture. Place second cake layer on top and spread with remainder of filling. Top with third cake layer. Refrigerate while preparing icing.

4. To make icing: gradually add 125 mL ($\frac{1}{2}$ cup) icing sugar to the egg white and beat well. Stir in almond extract and lemon juice. Slowly blend in more icing sugar until icing is thick enough to spread.

5. Ice the sides and top of cake evenly and decorate with grated chocolate, candied fruit and nuts.

Makes 10 to 12 servings

SAUCES

Although most people associate Italian sauces with the tomato, there are numerous other sauces, still popular, whose origins date much further back.

The Romans commonly used a fish-based concoction (*liquamen*) and two sauces made from the herbs silphium and asafetida, neither of which is still grown. Yet fish and herb sauces are used extensively in Italy even now and we include here some of the best.

The tomato did not appear in Europe until the fifteenth century. The Spaniards brought it from the New World in the form of a cherry-sized yellow fruit called "the golden apple." It soon became very popular and the French began calling it *pomme d'amour*, or "apple of love," believing it to be an aphrodisiac. Today the tomato occupies a permanent place in the hearts of the Italian people.

Tomato Pulp
POLPA DI POMODORO

If fresh tomatoes are out of season, you can use canned tomatoes, but make sure they are thoroughly drained and squeezed to get rid of all the seeds and excess moisture.

2–2.5 kg tomatoes	5 pounds

1. Place tomatoes in a large pot of boiling water and cook 3 to 5 minutes. Remove from pot, skin and cut in half.

2. Squeeze gently and remove seeds and juice.

3. Chop tomatoes finely and let stand in a bowl for about 20 minutes. Drain thoroughly and use as directed.

Makes about 1 L (1 quart)

Nut Sauce

SUGO DI NOCE

A little of this rich, earthy sauce gives a wonderful flavor to pasta.

60	g	shelled walnuts	2 ounces
75	mL	light cream	5 tablespoons
		Salt and freshly ground pepper	
		Leaves from 2 sprigs of marjoram, finely chopped,	
		OR 30 mL fresh chopped parsley	2 tablespoons

1. Coarsely chop or grind walnuts, then pound to a paste with a pestle in a mortar or pulverize in an electric blender.

2. Stir in cream, a little at a time, to form a sauce the consistency of thick cream. Add salt and pepper to taste and marjoram leaves or parsley.

3. Place sauce in blender and blend at medium speed for about 2 minutes. Serve over 250 g ($\frac{1}{2}$ pound) of hot buttered pasta.

Makes 2 to 3 servings

Bolognese Meat Sauce

POLPETTE DI CARNE ALLA BOLOGNESE

45	mL	sweet butter	3 tablespoons
60	g	lean prosciutto, diced OR salt pork, diced	2 ounces
125	mL	chopped onions	$\frac{1}{2}$ cup
90	mL	grated carrot	$\frac{1}{3}$ cup
90	mL	chopped celery	$\frac{1}{3}$ cup
150	g	ground beef	$\frac{1}{3}$ pound
150	g	ground pork	$\frac{1}{3}$ pound
150	g	ground veal	$\frac{1}{3}$ pound
30	mL	dried Italian mushrooms, soaked in tepid water for 20 minutes, squeezed dry and chopped	2 tablespoons
375	mL	dry red wine	$1\frac{1}{2}$ cups
30	mL	fresh chopped parsley	2 tablespoons
		Pinch each of marjoram, salt, freshly ground pepper and freshly grated OR ground nutmeg	
8	mL	all-purpose flour	$1\frac{1}{2}$ teaspoons

1		can (800 mL) plum tomatoes, drained (with seeds removed) and chopped	(28 ounces)
500	mL	beef broth	2 cups
125	mL	heavy cream (optional)	½ cup

1. In a large saucepan, melt butter and sauté prosciutto over low heat until browned. Add onions, carrot and celery and cook until onions are golden, stirring frequently (about 6 to 7 minutes).

2. Combine ground beef, pork and veal and mix well. Add meat and mushrooms to saucepan and increase heat to moderate; cook for 2 minutes, stirring constantly.

3. Add wine, parsley, marjoram, salt, pepper and nutmeg. Stir and cook until wine is almost evaporated.

4. Remove from heat and slowly blend in flour. Return to heat and cook 1 to 2 minutes, then add chopped tomato.

5. Gradually stir in beef broth and continue cooking on low heat, uncovered, for 1 hour. If desired, heavy cream can be stirred into sauce before serving. Serve with pasta, rice, potatoes, gnocchi or use in baked pasta dishes.

Makes 750 mL to 1 L (3 to 4 cups)

Syracuse Wine Sauce

RAGU AL VINO BIANCO

This sauce is excellent over cold tongue, fish or cold cuts.

625	mL	Moscato wine	2½ cups
125	mL	raisins	½ cup
2		whole cloves	
		Pinch of cinnamon	
6		egg yolks, beaten	

1. In a saucepan combine wine, raisins, cloves and cinnamon and gently boil until reduced to half.

2. Strain and cool.

3. Gradually whisk yolks into wine mixture and place in top part of double boiler over boiling water. Cook until slightly thickened, stirring often. Serve hot or cold.

Makes 375 to 500 mL (1½ to 2 cups)

Easy Tomato Sauce

SUGO DI POMODORO

This basic tomato sauce is simple to make and can be used in countless Italian dishes.

45–60	mL	olive oil	3–4 tablespoons
2		onions, sliced	
1		garlic clove	
		Sprig of fresh basil	
		OR pinch of dry basil	
1		can (800 g) tomatoes, strained through a sieve	(28 ounces)
		Pinch of sugar (optional)	
		Salt and freshly ground pepper	
30	mL	dry white wine (optional)	2 tablespoons

1. Heat oil and fry onions and garlic until golden brown (about 10 minutes).

2. Add basil and tomatoes. Simmer uncovered until sauce thickens stirring frequently (1 hour).

3. Discard garlic and add a pinch of sugar if sauce is too sharp.

4. Add salt and pepper to taste and, if desired, white wine.

Makes 1 L (1 quart)

White Sauce (Béchamel)

BESCIAMELLA

625	mL	milk	2½ cups
60	mL	butter	4 tablespoons
75	mL	all-purpose flour	5 tablespoons
		Salt and freshly ground pepper	
		Pinch of grated nutmeg	

1. Heat milk until little bubbles start to form around the edge. Do not boil. (If you want a thinner béchamel, add another 125 mL (½ cup) of milk.)

2. In a small saucepan, melt butter over low heat. With a wooden spoon, stir in flour and continue stirring over low heat until mixture (roux) no longer sticks to the sides of the pan (about 3 minutes).

3. Remove roux from heat and slowly add milk, beating well to form a smooth sauce.

4. Return to heat and stir until almost boiling. Reduce heat and simmer for 15 minutes. Season with salt and pepper to taste and nutmeg.

Makes about 750 mL (3 cups)

Tomato Purée
CONCENTRATO DI POMODORO

This purée is used as the base of several favorite tomato sauces.

2	kg	firm ripe tomatoes	4 pounds
		Boiling water	
10	mL	salt	2 teaspoons
45	mL	finely chopped onion	3 tablespoons
1		large bay leaf	

1. Place tomatoes in a large pot of boiling water with the heat turned off for 3 to 5 minutes. Peel and cut in half. Squeeze gently to remove seeds and juice. Sprinkle the inside with salt to draw out excess liquid.

2. Finely chop tomatoes and let stand in a bowl for 20 minutes. Drain thoroughly.

3. Place tomatoes in a saucepan with onion and bay leaf. Heat to a boil, then cook uncovered over moderate heat for 30 minutes, stirring occasionally at first but more frequently as sauce thickens.

4. Remove from heat, discard bay leaf and purée in blender.

Makes 2 to 3 cups

Genovese Green Sauce
PESTO ALLA GENOVESE

When Godfrey de Bouillon was on the first crusade to the holy land, he wrote in his diary, "Every evening at dinner time, there comes a fragrance of garlic and basil from a certain part of the camp, that part being the quarters of the Genoese." Such is the use of pesto *by the people of Genoa. Wonderful on chilled meats or cold pasta and it only takes a few minutes to make.*

125	mL	pine nuts OR walnuts	½ cup
60	mL	fresh chopped basil	4 tablespoons
30	mL	chopped raw spinach	2 tablespoons
10	mL	finely minced garlic	2 teaspoons
60	mL	grated Parmesan cheese	4 tablespoons
60	mL	grated Romano cheese	4 tablespoons
90	mL	butter, softened	6 tablespoons
125	mL	olive oil	½ cup
		Salt and freshly ground pepper	

1. Combine all ingredients in a mixing bowl and mix well.

2. Place mixture in an electric blender and whirl until smooth and creamy.

Makes 250 to 375 mL (1 to 1½ cups)

Cold Tomato Sauce
SALSA FREDDA DI POMODORO

This sauce is excellent with cold meats, fish and poultry as well as cold pasta.

750	mL	finely chopped tomato pulp (see page 99) OR canned plum tomatoes that have been thoroughly squeezed and drained	3 cups
1		garlic clove	
		Pinch of ground sage	
5	mL	salt	1 teaspoon
		Pinch of freshly ground pepper	
30	mL	sweet butter, at room temperature	2 tablespoons

1. Place tomato pulp, garlic, sage, salt and pepper in the top of a double boiler. Cook without boiling, stirring until ingredients are blended well.

2. Add butter, a little at a time. Stir until well mixed. Remove from heat. Discard garlic and chill.

3. Taste for seasoning and purée briefly in blender.

Makes 1 L (1 quart)

SINGLE-COURSE DISHES

Italians reserve the elaborate multicourse banquets for special occasions. Their main meal, eaten at midday, is usually served in two courses: soup or pasta, followed by meat and vegetables. Omitted completely are the antipasti, separate salad and dessert.

Supper is often served in one course, which may consist of any of the dishes in this section, with perhaps a salad, bread and cheese. Only in the faster-paced commercial centers is the main meal eaten in the evening.

Eggs Florentine
UOVA ALLA FIORENTINA

700	g	fresh spinach	1½ pounds
45	mL	olive oil	3 tablespoons
		Salt and freshly ground pepper	
4		eggs	
60	mL	grated Romano cheese	4 tablespoons

1. Preheat oven to 180°C (350°F).

2. Wash and drain the spinach carefully.

3. Heat oil in a saucepan and add spinach. Cover and cook until tender. Drain. Add salt and pepper to taste.

4. Arrange spinach in four individual baking dishes or ramekins. Break an egg over each serving of spinach and sprinkle with grated Romano cheese.

5. Bake until egg white is firm but yolk is still soft (about 3 minutes).

Makes 4 servings

Poached Eggs in Pea Sauce

UOVA E PISELLI

Try this served on toast or fried bread.

4	green onions, chopped	
	Oil for frying	
1	can (800 mL) tomatoes	(28 ounces)
1	can (400 mL) peas, drained	(14 ounces)
	Salt and freshly ground pepper	
6	eggs	

1. Sauté onions in oil until soft. Add tomatoes and simmer uncovered about 20 minutes.

2. Add peas, salt and pepper to taste and simmer 15 minutes more.

3. Crack eggs into sauce, one at a time, being careful not to break yolks. Cover and cook until eggs are done.

Makes 6 servings

Stuffed Pizza Trousers

PIZZA RIPIENA

This is one of the oldest pizza recipes in history. It dates back well over 2,000 years.

DOUGH

1		package dry yeast	
		Warm water	
15	mL	oil	1 tablespoon
500	mL	all-purpose flour	2 cups
5	mL	salt	1 teaspoon
		Oil	

FILLING

100	g	mozzarella cheese	4 ounces
50	g	salami	2 ounces
50	g	cooked ham	2 ounces

SAUCE

250	mL	tomato sauce (see recipe, page 102) (optional)	1 cup

1. Combine yeast with warm water and oil according to package directions.

2. Combine flour and salt. Add the dissolved yeast and mix to a firm, pliable dough, or until dough no longer sticks to the sides of the bowl.

3. Turn onto a floured board. Knead and stretch the dough until smooth and elastic (about 6 minutes). Shape into a ball and place in an oiled bowl. Cover and allow to rise in a warm place until dough is doubled in size (about 30 to 60 minutes).

4. When dough has risen, preheat oven to 220°C (425°F).

5. Turn dough onto a board, knead gently and divide in three parts. Roll each piece into a 15-cm (6-inch) diameter circle and brush with a thin coat of oil.

6. Dice the cheese and cut salami and ham into thin strips. Divide evenly among the three circles.

7. Fold each circle into a half-moon, pressing edges firmly together and enclosing the stuffing securely.

8. Rub a small amount of oil on your hands and then over each stuffed pizza or *calzone*. Place on a greased baking sheet and bake until cooked (20 minutes). Eat "trousers" just as they come from the oven or cover with a thick tomato sauce that has been heated.

Makes 3 to 6 servings

Meat Loaf with Potato Filling
POLPETTONE DI CARNE CON PATATE

15	mL	fresh chopped parsley	1 tablespoon
500	mL	mashed potatoes	2 cups
500	g	lean ground beef	1 pound
		OR half beef, half veal	
250	mL	bread crumbs	1 cup
250	mL	grated Parmesan cheese	1 cup
2		eggs	
1		small onion, chopped	
		Salt and freshly ground pepper	
30–45	mL	olive oil	2–3 tablespoons
250	g	mozzarella cheese, sliced	½ pound

1. Preheat oven to 180°C (350°F).

2. Add 5 mL (1 teaspoon) of the parsley to mashed potatoes and mix.

3. In a separate bowl, mix together ground meat, 175 mL (¾ cup) of the bread crumbs, remaining parsley, Parmesan cheese, eggs, onion, salt and pepper to taste.

4. Brush a standard loaf pan with 15 mL (1 tablespoon) olive oil and then sprinkle evenly with remaining bread crumbs.

5. Place half the meat mixture in the pan, then the complete potato-parsley mixture. Follow with a layer of mozzarella cheese slices and top with remaining meat, closing edges tightly so that potatoes can't escape while cooking.

6. Brush with remaining oil and bake until done (about 25 minutes).

7. Cool for 5 minutes. Turn upside down onto a warm platter, slice and serve hot.

Makes 4 to 6 servings

Zucchini Pancake

FRITTELLE DI ZUCCHINE

350	g	diced unpeeled zucchini	¾ pound
		Boiling salted water	
20	mL	fresh white bread crumbs	1½ tablespoons
40	mL	milk	2½ tablespoons
45	mL	grated Parmesan cheese	3 tablespoons
1–2	mL	grated lemon peel	¼ teaspoon
		Pinch of sugar	
		Salt	
4		eggs	
30	mL	butter	2 tablespoons

1. Preheat broiler to highest setting.

2. Add zucchini to a small pot of boiling salted water and blanch for 3 minutes. Drain.

3. In a large mixing bowl, soak bread crumbs in milk for 5 minutes.

4. Stir in zucchini, cheese, lemon peel, sugar and salt to taste.

5. In a separate bowl, beat eggs with a whisk or fork until well beaten.

6. Heat butter in a large frying pan. Add eggs to zucchini mixture and cook over moderate heat until eggs are set at edges but still slightly moist in the centre (about 2 to 3 minutes).

7. Slide frying pan under broiler to brown the top (about 30 seconds).

8. Slice into quarters and serve immediately.

Makes 4 servings

Basic Pizza
PIZZA SEMPLICE

Pizza is usually identified with the south (Naples claims to have invented it), but in fact, all along the coast from Sicily to Marseilles, France, variations are found under different names, such as "sardenaira" and "pissaladiere." The original version consisted of baked dough topped simply with chopped garlic and olive oil. But through the years, variations have developed and today you can find pizza with any number of toppings, including tomato sauce, cheese, pepperoni, anchovies and mushrooms.

5	mL	sugar	1 teaspoon
1		package dry yeast	
175	mL	lukewarm water	¾ cup
500	mL	all-purpose flour	2 cups
		Pinch of salt	
15–30	mL	olive oil	1–2 tablespoons
		All-purpose flour for kneading	
		Olive oil	

1. Add the sugar, then the yeast, to lukewarm water. Mix to dissolve and let stand in a warm place (10 to 15 minutes).

2. Make dough by combining the flour, salt, oil and dissolved yeast. Place dough on a floured board and knead until smooth and elastic (about 15 to 20 minutes). Place dough in an oiled bowl, cover with a damp tea towel and place in a warm place to rise.

3. When dough has doubled in bulk (about 2 hours) punch it down to its original size.

4. Preheat oven to 230°C (450°F).

5. Roll dough with a rolling pin or stretch with your hands on a pizza tray or cookie sheet. Add desired toppings. (See page 110.)

6. Bake for 20 minutes or until edges are crisp.

Makes 4 servings

Suggested Toppings: Try all or any combination of these toppings on your pizza.

375	mL	tomato sauce (see recipe, page 102)	1½ cups
125	mL	sliced mushrooms	½ cup
250	mL	chopped olives	1 cup
30	mL	bacon bits	2 tablespoons
250	mL	grated Mozzarella cheese	1 cup
2		tomatoes, sliced	
1		small pepperoni, sliced	
½		green pepper, thinly sliced	
2		anchovy fillets, cut into small pieces	

Eggplant with Rice Casserole
MELANZANE E RISO IN CASSERUOLA

3		medium-sized eggplants	
		Olive oil	
5	mL	salt	1 teaspoon
500	mL	uncooked white rice	2 cups
3		fresh tomatoes, peeled and chopped	
250	mL	fresh ricotta cheese	1 cup
2		garlic cloves, finely chopped	
15	mL	fresh chopped basil	1 tablespoon
		Salt and freshly ground pepper	

1. Slice eggplants in half lengthwise and then crosswise in 1.5-cm (½-inch) slices.

2. Pour about 250 mL (1 cup) of olive oil in a small mixing bowl and add salt. Set aside.

3. Heat 125 mL (½ cup) of olive oil in a frying pan and keep the bottle of olive oil handy.

4. Dip eggplant slices into the cold olive oil and then fry them in the hot oil until one side is brown; then turn and brown the other side. Replenish oil as needed.

5. Preheat oven to 200°C (400°F).

6. Cook rice on top of stove according to package directions. When done, season with raw peeled tomatoes and fresh ricotta cheese. Then add garlic, chopped basil and salt and pepper to taste and mix.

7. Line a buttered casserole with a layer of rice; place a layer of eggplant

on top and repeat until ingredients are used up, finishing with a layer of eggplant. Place in oven and immediately turn heat off. Heat until hot and serve. Or chill and serve cold the next day.

Makes 6 servings

Eggs, Hunter's Style
UOVA ALLA CACCIATORA

4		chicken livers	
		Salt and freshly ground pepper	
45	mL	olive oil	3 tablespoons
15	mL	chopped onion	1 tablespoon
15	mL	tomato paste	1 tablespoon
60	mL	warm water	4 tablespoons
60	mL	dry sauterne wine	4 tablespoons
4		eggs	

1. Cut chicken livers in half and season with salt and pepper to taste.

2. Heat oil in a frying pan and sauté liver and onions for 5 minutes over low heat.

3. Blend together tomato paste and warm water and add to the chicken livers. Simmer uncovered for 5 minutes.

4. Add the sauterne and cook 3 more minutes, uncovered.

5. Carefully add one egg at a time to prevent yolks from breaking. Cover and cook 3 to 5 minutes or until whites are firm. Serve hot on toast.

Makes 4 servings

Spinach Pudding
PASTICCIO DI SPINACI

1	kg	spinach	2 pounds
60	mL	butter	4 tablespoons
300	mL	béchamel sauce (see recipe, page 102)	1¼ cups
150	mL	vegetable OR chicken broth	⅔ cup
250	g	ground veal	½ pound
		Salt and freshly ground pepper	
3		eggs, beaten	

1. Chop spinach and wash well. Cook until limp in a covered saucepan with only the water clinging to the leaves. Drain and cool.

2. Place spinach in a saucepan with 45 mL (3 tablespoons) of butter, béchamel sauce and broth and simmer, covered, for 5 minutes. Remove from heat.

3. Sauté veal in 15 mL (1 tablespoon) of butter until brown. Season with salt and pepper to taste.

4. Add the veal and eggs to spinach mixture. Place in top part of double boiler over simmering water and cook, covered, until set (about 30 minutes). Serve with vegetables.

Makes 4 servings

Potatoes Stuffed with Sausage
PATATE RIPIENE ALLA SALSICCIA

8		large potatoes	
375	g	Italian sausage, sweet or hot	¾ pound
2		slices of bread, soaked in water and squeezed dry	
75	mL	butter	5 tablespoons
15	mL	fresh chopped parsley	1 tablespoon
15	mL	potato stock	1 tablespoon
1		egg yolk	
		Salt	
		Pinch of freshly ground pepper (omit with hot sausage)	

1. Preheat oven to 200°C (400°F).

2. Parboil potatoes for 10 minutes. Drain, reserving 15 mL (1 table-spoon) of stock, and peel. Scoop out of each whole potato a deep hole for stuffing.

3. Skin sausage and combine with bread, 30 mL (2 tablespoons) of butter, parsley, potato stock and egg yolk. Mix well. Carefully stuff potatoes with sausage mixture.

4. Place potatoes in a greased baking dish. Dot with remaining butter and season with salt and pepper.

5. Bake 15 minutes and serve.

Makes 8 servings

Broiled Liver and Mushrooms

FEGATO CON FUNGHI ALLA GRIGLIA

500	g	calves' liver, sliced 2-cm thick	1 pound, ¾-inch
250	g	mushrooms	½ pound
1		large onion, cut into wedges	
60	mL	olive oil	4 tablespoons
30	mL	wine vinegar	2 tablespoons
5	mL	fresh chopped mint	1 teaspoon
		Salt and freshly ground pepper	
		8 skewers	

1. Preheat broiler to 140°C (300°F).

2. Cut liver slices into 4-cm (1½-inch) squares.

3. Trim stems off mushrooms.

4. String liver, mushroom caps and onion wedges on each of 8 skewers until all ingredients are used. Brush with a mixture of olive oil, vinegar and mint.

5. Place skewers on broiler rack and broil for 5 minutes, 10 cm (4 inches) from element. Brush with remaining oil and vinegar and broil for an additional minute. Season with salt and pepper to taste and serve sizzling hot.

Makes 4 servings

Potatoes with Prosciutto

PATATE AL PROSCIUTTO

6		medium-sized potatoes	
3	L	boiling salted water	3 quarts
45	mL	olive oil	3 tablespoons
125	g	prosciutto, chopped	¼ pound
1		onion, chopped	
		Pinch of garlic powder	
500	mL	tomato pulp (see recipe, page 99)	2 cups
250	mL	chicken broth	1 cup
		Salt and freshly ground pepper	
45	mL	fresh chopped parsley	3 tablespoons
45	mL	fresh chopped basil	3 tablespoons
30	mL	butter	2 tablespoons

1. Scrub potatoes and cook in their skins in boiling salted water until tender (about 25 to 30 minutes). Drain, peel and slice.

2. Heat olive oil in a saucepan and sauté prosciutto and onion until onion is golden brown, stirring frequently.

3. Mix in garlic powder, tomato pulp, chicken broth, potato slices and salt and pepper to taste. Cover and simmer over low heat until heated through.

4. Add parsley, basil and butter. Stir gently until well mixed and serve.

Makes 6 servings

INDEX

Note: numerals in italics refer
to the illustrations

2. Cool slightly and slowly add eggs and sugar, whisking constantly. Cook uncovered in top of double boiler over boiling water, stirring constantly, until mixture becomes thick and smooth.

3. Cool and freeze at least 4 hours. Serve in sherbet glasses topped with whipped cream.

Makes 4 servings

Marsala Custard
CREMA ZABAIONE AL MARSALA

Marsala custard, or zabaione, is one of the best-known Italian sweet puddings. It's delicious served hot or as a cold custard over fruit.

12		egg yolks	
150	mL	sugar	⅔ cup
		Pinch of cinnamon	
		Scraped vanilla bean (5 cm long)	(2 inches long)
		OR 10 ml vanilla extract	2 teaspoons
375	mL	dry Marsala wine	1½ cups

1. Beat together egg yolks, sugar, cinnamon and vanilla with a whisk or electric beater until smooth.

2. Place in top part of double boiler over boiling water and, constantly whisking, heat until mixture is frothy and pale yellow (2 to 3 minutes).

3. Gradually add Marsala wine, beating constantly, and continue heating until hot, but do not boil. Remove vanilla bean and serve hot; or allow to cool, refrigerate and serve cold.

Makes 4 to 6 servings

Lugano Apple Tart
TORTA DI MELE ALLA LUGANO

PASTRY

250	mL	all purpose flour	1 cup
		Pinch of salt	
185	mL	butter	¾ cup
2		egg yolks	
30	mL	cream	2 tablespoons

Honey Paste with Puff Pastry

PASTA DI MIELE IN PASTICCIO SOUFFLE

150	mL	all-purpose flour	⅔ cup
5	mL	baking powder	1 teaspoon
150	mL	ricotta cheese	⅔ cup
150	mL	butter OR margarine, softened	⅔ cup
5	mL	salt	1 teaspoon
		Honey	
125	mL	blanched slivered almonds	½ cup
50	mL	candied cherries	¼ cup

1. To make puff pastry: Sift together flour and baking powder into a mixing bowl. Add ricotta cheese, butter and salt and knead until smooth and elastic (about 15 minutes).

2. On a well-floured cloth, roll out dough, then work back into a ball, roll out again and work into a ball again. Wrap in waxed paper and refrigerate about 20 minutes.

3. Preheat oven to 190°C (375°F).

4. Roll out puff pastry very thin, about the size of a large pizza.

5. Coat pastry with desired amount of honey and top with blanched almonds and candied cherries. Roll up tightly and cut into finger-thick slices. Place on their side on a greased baking sheet and bake 15 minutes or until crisp and golden.

Makes 12 to 24 servings

Coffee Ice Cream

GELATO DI CREMA DI CAFFE

250	mL	strong espresso coffee	1 cup
500	mL	heavy cream	2 cups
4		eggs, beaten	
375	mL	sugar	1½ cups
		Whipped cream for topping	

1. Combine coffee and heavy cream. Heat until almost boiling. (Do not boil.)